Social Security A

CW00432813

CHAPTER 50

ARRANGEMENT OF SECTIONS

PART I

PENSIONS

A

ELIZABETH II

Social Security Act 1986

1986 CHAPTER 50

An Act to make provision in relation to personal pension schemes, to amend the law relating to social security, occupational pension schemes and the provision of refreshments for school pupils, to abolish maternity pay under the Employment Protection (Consolidation) Act 1978 and provide for the winding-up of the Maternity Pay Fund, to empower the Secretary of State to pay the travelling expenses of certain persons, and for connected purposes. *[25th July 1986]*

B E IT ENACTED by the Queen's most Excellent Majesty, by and with the advice and consent of the Lords Spiritual and Temporal, and Commons, in this present Parliament assembled, and by the authority of the same, as follows:—

PART I

PENSIONS

Personal pension schemes

1.—(1) Subject to the following provisions of this Part of this Act, the Secretary of State shall pay, except in such circumstances as may be prescribed, minimum contributions in respect of an employed earner for any period during which the earner—

Minimum contributions to personal pension schemes.

    (*a*) is over the age of 16 but has not attained pensionable age ;

    (*b*) is not a married woman or widow who has made an election which is still operative that her liability in respect of primary Class 1 contributions shall be a liability to contribute at a reduced rate ; and

(c) is a member of an appropriate personal pension scheme which is for the time being the earner's chosen scheme.

(2) Regulations may make provision as to the manner in which, and time at which or period within which, minimum contributions are to be paid.

(3) Subject to subsection (4) below, the Secretary of State shall pay minimum contributions in respect of an earner to the trustees or managers of the earner's chosen scheme.

(4) In such circumstances as may be prescribed the Secretary of State shall pay minimum contributions to a prescribed person.

(5) Where any of the conditions mentioned in subsections above ceases to be satisfied in the case of an earner in respect of whom the Secretary of State is required to pay minimum contributions, the duty of the Secretary of State to pay them shall cease as from a date determined in accordance with regulations.

(6) If the Secretary of State pays an amount by way of minimum contributions which he is not required to pay, he may recover it from the person to whom he paid it or from any person in respect of whom he paid it.

(7) If he pays in respect of an earner an amount by way of minimum contributions which he is required to pay, but does not pay it to the trustees or managers of the earner's chosen scheme, he may recover it from the person to whom he paid it or from the earner.

(8) A personal pension scheme is an appropriate scheme if there is in force a certificate (in this Act referred to as an " appropriate scheme certificate ") issued by the Occupational Pensions Board in accordance with section 2 below that it is such a scheme.

(9) Where an earner and the trustees or managers of an appropriate personal pension scheme have jointly given notice to the Secretary of State, in such manner and form and with such supporting evidence as may be prescribed—

(a) that the earner is, or intends to become, a member of the scheme and wishes minimum contributions in respect of him to be paid to the scheme ;

(b) that the trustees or managers have agreed to accept him as a member of the scheme and to receive minimum contributions in respect of him,

that scheme is the earner's chosen scheme as from a date determined in accordance with regulations and specified in the notice, unless at that date some other appropriate scheme is the earner's chosen scheme.

(10) Either an earner or the trustees or managers of a scheme may cancel a notice under subsection (9) above by giving notice to that effect to the Secretary of State at such time and in such manner and form as may be prescribed.

(11) Where a notice under subsection (10) above is given, the scheme ceases to be the earner's chosen scheme as from a date determined in accordance with regulations and specified in the notice.

2.—(1) Regulations shall provide—

    (a) for the issue of appropriate scheme certificates by the Occupational Pensions Board ;

    (b) for the cancellation, variation or surrender of any such certificate, or the issue of an amended certificate, on any relevant change of circumstances ; and

    (c) that any question whether a personal pension scheme is or at any time was an appropriate scheme shall be determined by the Board.

(2) A scheme can be an appropriate scheme only if the requirements imposed by or by virtue of Schedule 1 to this Act are satisfied in its case.

(3) An appropriate scheme certificate may be withheld or cancelled by the Board if they consider that there are circumstances which make it inexpedient that it should be or continue to be an appropriate scheme, notwithstanding that they would otherwise issue such a certificate or not cancel such a certificate.

(4) Where by or by virtue of any provision of Schedule 1 to this Act a scheme's being an appropriate scheme depends on the satisfaction of a particular condition, the scheme's continuing to be an appropriate scheme shall be dependent on continued satisfaction of the condition ; and if the condition ceases to be satisfied that shall be a ground (without prejudice to any other) for the cancellation or variation of an appropriate scheme certificate.

(5) Except in prescribed circumstances, no appropriate scheme certificate and no cancellation, variation or surrender of such a certificate shall have effect from a date earlier than that on which the certificate is issued or the cancellation, variation or surrender is made.

(6) An appropriate scheme certificate for the time being in force in relation to a scheme shall be conclusive that the scheme is an appropriate scheme.

(7) Every assignment of or charge on and every agreement to assign or charge protected rights or payments giving effect to protected rights shall be void.

(8) On the bankruptcy of a person who is entitled to protected rights or a payment giving effect to protected rights, any protected rights or payment the assignment of which is or would be made void by subsection (7) above shall not pass to any trustee or person acting on behalf of his creditors.

(9) In the application of this section to Scotland—

(*a*) references to assignment shall be construed as references to assignation and " assign " shall be construed accordingly ; and

(*b*) the reference to a person's bankruptcy shall be construed as a reference to the sequestration of his estate or the appointment on his estate of a judicial factor under section 41 of the Solicitors (Scotland) Act 1980.

1980 c. 46.

Amount of minimum contributions.
3.—(1) Subject to subsection (2) below, in relation to any tax week falling within a period for which the Secretary of State is required to pay minimum contributions in respect of an earner, the amount of those contributions shall be the aggregate of—

(*a*) the rebate percentage of so much of any earnings paid to or for the benefit of the earner with respect to any employment which is not contracted-out employment in relation to him as exceeds the lower earnings limit but does not exceed the upper earnings limit ; and

(*b*) where the tax week ends before 6th April 1993, 2 per cent. of any such earnings or, if 2 per cent. of any such earnings is less than £1·00 and the prescribed person applies within such time, in such form and manner and with such supporting evidence as may be prescribed, £1·00.

(2) In relation to earnings paid with respect to any such employment as may be prescribed, subsection (1) above shall have effect as if the words " the aggregate of " and paragraph (*b*) and the word " and " immediately preceding it were omitted.

(3) In subsection (1) above—

" employment " means employed earner's employment ; and

" rebate percentage " means the percentage arrived at by adding—

1975 c. 60.
(*a*) the percentage by which for the time being under section 27(2) of the Social Security Pensions Act 1975 the contracted-out percentage of primary Class 1 contributions is less than the normal percentage ; and

(*b*) the percentage by which for the time being under that subsection the contracted-out percentage of secondary Class 1 contributions is less than the normal percentage.

(4) **The** references to the upper and lower earnings limits in subsection (1)(*a*) above are references, in the case of an earner who is paid otherwise than weekly, to their prescribed equivalents under section 4(2) and (6) of the Social Security Act 1975.

(5) Regulations may provide—

(*a*) that earnings shall be calculated or estimated in such manner and on such basis as may be prescribed for the purpose of determining whether any, and if so what, minimum contributions are payable in respect of them ;

(*b*) for the adjustment of the amount which would otherwise be payable by way of minimum contributions so as to avoid the payment of trivial or fractional amounts ;

(*c*) for the intervals at which, for the purposes of minimum contributions, payments of earnings are to be treated as made ;

(*d*) for this section to have effect, in prescribed cases, as if for any reference to a tax week there were substituted a reference to a prescribed period and as if in any case so prescribed for the references to £1·00 in subsection (1)(*b*) above there were substituted references to such other sum as may be prescribed.

4.—(1) Where for any period minimum contributions have been paid in respect of an earner, sections 16(2B), 28(7A) and 59 (1A) of the Social Security Act 1975 and section 29 of the Social Security Pensions Act 1975 shall have effect—

(*a*) in relation to him, as from the date on which he reaches pensionable age, as if he were entitled to a guaranteed minimum pension at a prescribed weekly rate arising from that period ;

(*b*) in prescribed circumstances, in relation to any widow or widower of the earner—

(i) if the earner died after reaching pensionable age, as if the widow or widower were entitled to a guaranteed minimum pension at a rate equal to one-half of the rate prescribed under paragraph (*a*) above ; and

(ii) if the earner died before reaching pensionable age, as if the widow or widower were entitled to a guaranteed minimum pension at a prescribed weekly rate arising from that period.

(2) **The** power to prescribe a rate conferred by subsection (1) (*a*) above includes power to prescribe a nil rate.

5.—(1) In the case of a personal pension scheme which is or has been an appropriate scheme the Occupational Pensions Board may, for the event of, or in connection with, its ceasing to be an appropriate scheme, approve any arrangements made or to be made in relation to the scheme, or for its purposes, for the preservation or transfer of protected rights under the scheme.

(2) If the scheme ceases to be an appropriate scheme (whether by being wound up or otherwise) and the Board either—

(a) have withdrawn their approval of previously approved arrangements relating to it ; or

(b) have declined to approve arrangements relating to it,

the Board may issue a certificate to that effect.

(3) A certificate issued under subsection (2)(a) or (b) above shall be cancelled by the Board if they subsequently approve the arrangements.

(4) If the scheme ceases to be an appropriate scheme (whether by being wound up or otherwise), a state scheme premium shall be payable, except in prescribed circumstances—

(a) in respect of each earner whose protected rights under the scheme are not subject to approved arrangements ; and

(b) in respect of each person who has become entitled to receive a pension under the scheme giving effect to protected rights which are not subject to approved arrangements.

(5) A premium under subsection (4) above may be referred to as a " personal pension protected rights premium ".

1975 c. 60. (6) If at any time regulations are in force by virtue of which section 52C of or paragraph 16 of Schedule 1A to the Social Security Pensions Act 1975 has effect in relation to personal pension schemes, subsection (4)(a) above shall have effect as if after the word " arrangements " there were inserted the words " and have not been disposed of so as to discharge the trustees or managers of the scheme under section 52C of or paragraph 16 of Schedule 1A to the Social Security Pensions Act 1975 ".

(7) A personal pension protected rights premium shall be paid by the prescribed person, within the prescribed period, to the Secretary of State.

(8) The amount of a personal pension protected rights premium payable in respect of any person shall be the cash equivalent of the protected rights in question, calculated and verified in the prescribed manner.

(9) Where a personal pension protected rights premium is paid in respect of a person—

(a) the rights whose cash equivalent is included in the premium shall be extinguished ; and

(b) section 4 above and section 29(2) and (2A) of the Social Security Pensions Act 1975 shall have effect in relation to that person and a widow or widower of that person as if any guaranteed minimum pension to which that person or any such widow or widower is treated as entitled under those provisions and which derives from the minimum contributions, minimum payments (within the meaning of the Social Security Pensions Act 1975) or transfer payment or payments from which those rights derive were reduced by the appropriate percentage.

(10) In subsection (9) above " the appropriate percentage " means, subject to the following provisions of this section, $\frac{X}{Y} \times 100$, where—

> (a) X = the amount of the premium together with, if the person in respect of whom it falls to be paid gives notice to the prescribed person within the prescribed period—
>
>> (i) the cash equivalent, calculated and verified in the prescribed manner and paid to the Secretary of State within the prescribed period, of any other rights which he has under the scheme and specifies in the notice ; and
>>
>> (ii) the amount of any voluntary contribution paid to the Secretary of State within the prescribed period by, or in respect of, the person concerned ; and
>
> (b) Y = the cost of providing any guaranteed minimum pension such as is mentioned in subsection (9) above.

(11) If the appropriate percentage, as calculated under subsection (10) above, would fall between two whole numbers, it is to be taken to be the lower number.

(12) If it would be over 100, it is to be taken to be 100.

(13) The remainder after the reduction for which subsection (9) above provides—

> (a) if it would contain a fraction of 1p, is to be treated as the nearest lower whole number of pence ; and
>
> (b) if it would be less than a prescribed amount, is to be treated as nil.

(14) The power to make regulations conferred by subsections (8) and (10) above includes power to provide that cash equivalents are to be calculated and verified in such manner as may be approved in particular cases—

> (a) by prescribed persons ;
>
> (b) by persons with prescribed professional qualifications or experience ; or

(c) by persons approved by the Secretary of State,

and power to provide that they shall be calculated and verified in accordance with guidance prepared by a prescribed body.

(15) The cost of providing the appropriate percentage of the guaranteed minimum pension shall be certified by the Secretary of State, and in calculating and certifying it the Secretary of State—

>   (a) shall apply whichever of the prescribed actuarial tables (as in force at the time when the scheme ceases to be appropriate) is applicable in accordance with the regulations prescribing the tables ; and

>   (b) may make such adjustments as he thinks necessary for avoiding fractional amounts.

Occupational pension schemes

Money purchase contracted-out schemes.

1975 c. 60.

6. Schedule 2 to this Act has effect to make amendments of the Social Security Pensions Act 1975 in relation to the contracting-out of schemes which provide money purchase benefits.

Schemes becoming contracted-out between 1986 and 1993.

7.—(1) Subject to subsection (3) below and except in such cases as may be prescribed, where an occupational pension scheme becomes a contracted-out scheme under Part III of the Social Security Pensions Act 1975 during the period beginning on 1st January 1986 and ending on 5th April 1993, having not previously been contracted-out during any part of that period, the Secretary of State shall make in relation to any tax week falling within the period beginning on 6th April 1988 and ending on 5th April 1993 a payment under this section in respect of each earner who is in employment which—

>   (a) is contracted-out by reference to the scheme during that tax week ; and

>   (b) has not previously been contracted-out employment by reference to any other scheme during any part of the period beginning on 1st January 1986 and ending on 5th April 1993.

(2) The Secretary of State shall make a payment under this section to the trustees or managers of the scheme except that in such circumstances as may be prescribed he shall make such a payment to a prescribed person.

(3) A payment under this section shall not be made unless the prescribed person makes a claim for it in such manner and form, and at such time or within such period, as may be prescribed.

(4) The amount of a payment under this section in respect of a tax week is—

(a) 2 per cent. of so much of any earnings paid to or for the benefit of the earner in respect of the employment which is contracted-out by reference to the scheme in the tax week as exceeds the lower earnings limit for that week but does not exceed the upper earnings limit for it ; or

(b) if 2 per cent. of any such earnings is less than £1·00, £1·00.

(5) The references to the upper and lower earnings limits in subsection (4) above are references, in the case of an earner who is paid otherwise than weekly, to their prescribed equivalents under section 4(2) and (6) of the Social Security Act 1975.

(6) Regulations may make provision—

(a) for earnings to be calculated or estimated in such manner and on such basis as may be prescribed for the purpose of determining whether any, and if so what, payments under this section are to be made in respect of them ;

(b) for the adjustment of amounts which would otherwise be the amounts of payments under this section so as to avoid the payment of fractional amounts ;

(c) for the intervals at which, for the purposes of payments under this section, payments of earnings are to be treated as made ;

(d) for this section to have effect, in prescribed cases, as if for any reference to a tax week there were substituted a reference to a prescribed period and as if in any case so prescribed for the references to £1·00 in subsection (4)(b) above there were substituted references to such other sum as may be prescribed ; and

(e) as to the manner in which, and time at which or period within which, payments under this section are to be made.

(7) Where in the case of a scheme a payment has been made under this section in relation to an earner—

(a) if a premium is paid under section 42 of the Social Security Pensions Act 1975 in relation to him, the amount of the premium shall be increased by the amount of the payment ; and

(b) if a premium is paid under section 44 or 44A of that Act in relation to him, the amount of the premium shall be increased by the amount of the payment and by a further amount representing interest on the payment and calculated in accordance with regulations.

(8) If the Secretary of State makes a payment under this section which he is not required to make, he may recover the

PART I

amount of the payment from the person to whom he paid it, or from any person in respect of whom he paid it.

(9) If he makes in respect of an earner a payment under this section which he is required to make, but does not make it to the trustees or managers to whom he is required to make it, he may recover the amount of the payment from the person to whom he paid it or from the earner.

Abolition of requirement relating to requisite benefits. 1975 c. 60.

8. The requirement of the Social Security Pensions Act 1975 that for an occupational pension scheme to be contracted-out in relation to an earner's employment it must provide requisite benefits shall cease except so far as it relates to guaranteed minimum pensions and except to that extent shall be treated for the purposes of section 50 of that Act (requirement of consent of Occupational Pensions Board to alterations of rules of schemes) as if it had never existed.

Guaranteed minimum pensions.

9.—(1) The following subsection shall be substituted for sub-section (3) of section 35 of the Social Security Pensions Act 1975 (earner's guaranteed minimum)—

" (3) In subsection (2) above—
" the appropriate percentage " means—

(a) in respect of the earner's earnings factors for any tax year not later than the tax year 1987-88—

(i) if the earner was not more than 20 years under pensionable age on 6th April 1978, $1\frac{1}{4}$ per cent. ;

(ii) in any other case $\frac{25}{N}$ per cent. ;

(b) in respect of the earner's earnings factors for the tax year 1988-89 and for subsequent tax years—

(i) if the earner was not more than 20 years under pensionable age on 6th April 1978, 1 per cent. ;

(ii) in any other case $\frac{20}{N}$ per cent. ;

where N is the number of years in the earner's working life (assuming he will attain pensionable age) which fall after 5th April 1978 ; and—
" derived " means derived in accordance with the rules to be embodied in regulations.".

(2) The following subsections shall be inserted after subsection (6) of that section—

" (6A) Where an earner's guaranteed minimum pension is increased under subsection (6) above, the increase of that part of it which is attributable to earnings factors for the

tax year 1987-88 and earlier tax years shall be calculated separately from the increase of the rest.

(6B) Where one or more orders have come into force under section 37A below during the period for which the commencement of a guaranteed minimum pension is postponed, the amount of the pension for any week in that period shall be determined as if the order or orders had come into force before the beginning of the period.".

(3) In section 36 of that Act (widows)—

(*a*) the following subsections shall be substituted for subsection (1)—

" (1) Subject to the provisions of this Part of this Act, for an occupational pension scheme to be contracted-out in relation to an earner's employment it must provide, in the event of the earner dying (whether before or after attaining pensionable age) and leaving a widow or widower, for the widow or widower to be entitled to a guaranteed minimum pension under the scheme.

(1A) A scheme need not provide for widowers of earners who die before 6th April 1989 to be entitled to guaranteed minimum pensions." ;

(*b*) the following subsection shall be substituted for subsection (3)—

" (3) To comply with this section the scheme must also contain a rule to the effect that—

(*a*) if the earner is a man who had a guaranteed minimum under section 35 above, the weekly rate of the widow's pension will be not less than her guaranteed minimum, which shall be half that of the earner :

(*b*) if the earner is a woman who had such a guaranteed minimum, the weekly rate of the widower's pension will be not less than his guaranteed minimum, which shall be one-half of that part of the earner's guaranteed minimum which is attributable to earnings factors for the tax year 1988-89 and subsequent tax years." ; and

(*c*) the following subsections shall be inserted after subsection (7)—

" (7A) The scheme must provide for the widower's pension to be payable in prescribed circumstances and for the prescribed period.

(7B) The trustees or managers of the scheme shall supply to the Secretary of State any such information as he may require relating to the payment of pensions under the scheme to widowers.".

(4) The following provisions of that Act shall be construed as if the references to " widow " included references to " widower "—

(*a*) section 26(2) ;

(*b*) section 32(2)(*a*) ;

(*c*) section 36(8) ;

(*d*) section 38(3) ;

(*e*) section 39(4)(*b*) ;

(*f*) section 41B(1)(*c*), (2)(*a*) and (*b*) and (3) ;

(*g*) section 44(9) ;

(*h*) section 52D,

and with consequential modifications.

(5) The reference in section 29(1) of that Act to a person entitled to a guaranteed minimum pension shall be construed as including a reference to a person so entitled by virtue of being the widower of an earner in any case where he is entitled to a widower's invalidity pension, but that reference shall be so construed where he is entitled to any other benefit only if—

(*a*) at the time of the earner's death she and her husband had both attained pensionable age ; or

(*b*) he is also entitled to a Category A retirement pension by virtue of section 16(5) of that Act.

(6) The following provisions of that Act shall be construed as if the references to a person entitled to receive a guaranteed minimum pension included references to a person so entitled by virtue of being the widower of an earner only in such cases as may be prescribed—

(*a*) section 44(1)(*b*) and (2)(*b*) ; and

(*b*) section 49(1) ; and

(*c*) section 50(3) ;

and the references to " widow " in section 44(5) of that Act shall be construed as including references to " widower ", and the reference in section 49(6) of that Act to guaranteed minimum pensions as including a reference to the guaranteed minimum pension of such a person, only in those cases.

(7) The following section shall be inserted after section 37 of that Act—

" Annual increases of guaranteed minimum pensions.

37A.—(1) The Secretary of State shall in the tax year 1989-90 review the general level of prices obtaining in Great Britain for a period of twelve months commencing in the previous tax year.

(2) The Secretary of State shall in each subsequent tax year review the general level of prices obtaining

in Great Britain for the period of twelve months
commencing at the end of the period last reviewed
under this section.

(3) Where it appears to the Secretary of State that
the general level of prices is greater at the end of
the period under review than it was at the beginning
of that period, he shall lay before Parliament the
draft of an order specifying a percentage by which
there is to be an increase of the rate of that part of
guaranteed minimum pensions which is attributable
to earnings factors for the tax year 1988-89 and
subsequent tax years for—

    (*a*) earners who have attained pensionable age ;
       and

    (*b*) widows and widowers.

(4) The percentage shall be—

    (*a*) the percentage by which the general level
       of prices is greater at the end of the period
       under review than it was at the beginning
       of that period ; or

    (*b*) 3 per cent.,

whichever is less.

(5) If a draft order laid before Parliament in pursuance of this section is approved by a resolution of
each House, the Secretary of State shall make the
order in the form of the draft.

(6) An order under this section shall be so framed
as to bring the alterations to which it relates into
force on the first day of the tax year next following
the making of the order.

(7) Where the benefits mentioned in sections
16(2B), 28(7A) and 59(1A) of the Social Security 1975 c. **14.**
Act 1975 and section 29(1) above are not increased
on the day on which an order under this section
takes effect, the order shall be treated for the purposes of those subsections as not taking effect until
the day on which the benefits mentioned in them
are next increased.

(8) Except as permitted by subsection (13), (14) or
(15) below, the trustees or managers of a scheme may
not make an increase in a person's pension which is
required by virtue of this section out of money which
would otherwise fall to be used for the payment of

benefits under the scheme to or in respect of that person unless—

(*a*) the payment is to an earner in respect of the tax year in which he attains pensionable age and the increase is the one required to be made in the following year ; or

(*b*) the payment is to a person as the widow or widower of an earner who died before attaining pensionable age in respect of the tax year in which the person became a widow or widower and the increase is the one required to be made in the next following tax year.

(9) Subsection (8) above overrides any provision of a scheme to the extent that it conflicts with it.

(10) The Occupational Pensions Board may at any time, and shall if requested by the trustees and managers of a scheme, advise on any question whether or not subsection (8) above overrides any provision of the scheme.

(11) On an application made to them in respect of a scheme (other than a public service pension scheme) by persons competent to make such an application in respect of it, the Board shall issue a determination on any such question as is mentioned in subsection (10) above.

(12) The persons competent to make an application under subsection (11) above in respect of a scheme are—

(*a*) the trustees or managers of the scheme ;

(*b*) any person other than the trustees or managers who has power to alter any of the rules of the scheme ;

(*c*) any person who was an employer of persons in service in an employment to which the scheme applies ;

(*d*) any member or prospective member of the scheme ; and

(*e*) such other persons as may be prescribed, in relation to any category of schemes into which the scheme falls, as being proper persons to make an application for the purposes of this section in respect of a scheme of that category.

(13) Where in the tax year 1989-90 the trustees or managers of an occupational pension scheme make an increase in the rate of pensions currently payable to the members of the scheme who have attained pensionable age or to the widows or widowers of members, they may deduct the amount of the increase from any increase which, but for this subsection, they would be required to make under this section in the tax year 1990-91.

(14) Where the trustees or managers of such a scheme make an increase otherwise than in pursuance of this section in a tax year subsequent to 1989-90, they may deduct the amount of the increase from any increase which, but for this subsection, they would be required to make under this section in the next following tax year.

(15) Where in any tax year subsequent to 1989-90 the trustees or managers of a scheme make an increase which is partly made otherwise than in pursuance of this section, they may deduct the part of the increase made otherwise than in pursuance of this section from any increase which, but for this subsection, they would be required to make under this section in the next following year.

(16) Where by virtue of subsection (13), (14) or (15) above guaranteed minimum pensions are not required to be increased in pursuance of this section, their amount shall be calculated for any purpose as if they had been so increased.

(17) Where by virtue of any of those subsections guaranteed minimum pensions are required to be increased in pursuance of this section by an amount less than they otherwise would be, their amount shall be calculated for any purpose as if they had been increased by that full amount.".

(8) In section 59 of that Act (increase of official pensions) the following subsection shall be inserted after subsection (5)—

" (5A) Nothing in section 37A(13), (14) or (15) above authorises any deduction from an increase in the rate of an official pension under this section.".

(9) In section 59A of that Act (modification of effect of section 59(5)) the following subsection shall be inserted after subsection (2)—

" (2A) Where in any tax year—

(*a*) an increase is calculated in accordance with a direction under this section ; and

(*b*) the amount by reference to which the increase is calculated, or any part of it, is increased in that tax year under section 37A above,

the increase calculated in accordance with the direction shall be reduced by the amount of the increase under section 37A above.".

Short-service benefit: qualifying service.

1973 c. 38.

10. In paragraphs 6(1)(*b*) and 7 of Schedule 16 to the Social Security Act 1973 (preservation of benefits under occupational pension scheme) for " 5 " wherever occurring there shall be substituted " 2 ".

Auditors.

1975 c. 60.

11. The following shall be inserted after section 56N of the Social Security Pensions Act 1975—

" *Auditors*

Regulations as to auditors

56P. The Secretary of State may by regulations make provision as to—

(*a*) the appointment, resignation and removal of auditors of occupational pension schemes ;

(*b*) the duty of employers and auditors of employers to disclose information to the trustees or managers of occupational pension schemes and the auditors of such schemes ;

(*c*) the duty of trustees or managers of an occupational pension scheme to disclose information and to make available documents to the auditors of the scheme.".

Provisions applying to personal and occupational pension schemes

Voluntary contributions.

12.—(1) Except in such cases as may be prescribed, and except so far as is necessary to ensure that a personal or occupational pension scheme has, or may be expected to qualify for, tax-exemption or tax-approval, the rules of the scheme—

(*a*) must not prohibit, or allow any person to prohibit, the payment by a member of voluntary contributions ;

(*b*) must not impose, or allow any person to impose, any upper or lower limit on the payment by a member of voluntary contributions ;

(*c*) must secure that any voluntary contributions paid by a member are to be used by the trustees or managers of the scheme to provide additional benefits for or in respect of him ; and (*d*) must secure that the value of the additional benefits is reasonable, having regard—

> (i) to the amount of the voluntary contributions; and

> (ii) to the value of the other benefits under the scheme;

and the requirements specified in this subsection may be referred to as " the voluntary contributions requirements ".

(2) Where the rules of a personal or occupational pension scheme do not comply with the voluntary contributions requirements it shall be the responsibility of—

(*a*) the trustees and managers of the scheme; or

(*b*) in the case of a public service pension scheme, the Minister, government department or other person or body concerned with its administration,

to take such steps as are open to them for bringing the rules of the scheme into conformity with those requirements.

(3) The Occupational Pensions Board may at any time, and shall if requested by any such persons as are mentioned in subsection (2) above, advise whether the rules of a scheme do or do not in the Board's opinion conform with the voluntary contributions requirements and, where the Board advise that the rules do not conform, they shall indicate what steps they consider should be taken with a view to securing conformity.

(4) On application made to them in respect of a personal or occupational pension scheme (other than a public service pension scheme) by persons competent to make such an application in respect of it, the Occupational Pensions Board shall issue a determination as to whether or not the rules of the scheme conform with the voluntary contributions requirements.

(5) The persons competent to make an application under this section in respect of a scheme are—

(*a*) the trustees or managers of the scheme;

(*b*) any person other than the trustees or managers who has power to alter any of the rules of the scheme;

(*c*) in the case of an occupational pension scheme, any person who is an employer of persons in service in an employment to which the scheme applies;

(*d*) any member or prospective member of the scheme;

(*e*) such other persons as may be prescribed, in relation to any category of schemes into which the scheme falls, as being proper persons to make an application for the purposes of this section in respect of a scheme of that category.

(6) The Board may at any time of their own motion issue in respect of a scheme which has come to their notice any determination which they could issue in the case of that scheme on an application made to them under subsection (4) above.

(7) If the Occupational Pensions Board determine under subsection (4) or (6) above that the rules of a scheme do not conform with the voluntary contributions requirements they shall, either at the time of issuing their determination or as soon thereafter as they think expedient—

> (a) by order direct the trustees or managers of the scheme, or any such persons as are referred to in subsection (5)(b) above, to exercise such powers as they possess for modifying the scheme with a view to bringing it into conformity with those requirements (for which purpose the Board shall include in their order such directions as they think appropriate to indicate the modification appearing to them to be called for) ; or

> (b) if there is no person with power to modify the scheme as required by the Board, by order authorise the trustees or managers, or other persons named in the order (who in relation to an occupational pension scheme may in particular include such an employer as is specified in subsection (5)(c) above), to make that modification ; or

> (c) themselves by order modify the scheme with a view to achieving the purpose above-mentioned.

(8) The Board may exercise their powers under subsection (7) above from time to time in relation to any scheme in respect of which they have issued a determination under subsection (4) or (6) above, and may exercise the powers together or separately.

(9) Any modification of a scheme made in pursuance of an order of the Board under subsection (7)(b) or (c) above shall be as effective in law as if it had been made under powers conferred by or under the scheme ; and such an order may be made and complied with in relation to a scheme—

> (a) notwithstanding any enactment or rule of law, or any rule of the scheme, which would otherwise operate to prevent the modification being made ;

> (b) without regard to any such enactment, rule of law or rule of the scheme as would otherwise require, or might otherwise be taken to require, the implementation of any procedure, or of the obtaining of any consent, with a view to the making of the modification.

(10) An order of the Board under subsection (7)(a) above may require persons to exercise a power retrospectively

(whether or not the power could otherwise be so exercised), and an order under subsection (7)(*b*) or (*c*) above may operate retrospectively; and in this subsection " retrospectively " means with effect from the date before that on which the power is exercised or, as the case may be, the order is made, not being in either case a date earlier than the coming into operation of this section.

(11) In section 64(3) of the Social Security Act 1973 (modification and winding up by order of Occupational Pensions Board) the following paragraph shall be inserted after paragraph (*f*)—

" (*g*) to comply with the voluntary contributions requirements specified in subsection (1) of section 12 of the Social Security Act 1986, but without prejudice to anything in subsections (2) to (10) of that section,".

13. Regulations may be made relating to the form and content of advertisements and such other material as may be prescribed issued by or on behalf of the trustees or managers of a personal or occupational pension scheme for the purposes of the scheme.

14. Regulations may require the furnishing by prescribed persons to the Secretary of State or the Occupational Pensions Board of such information as he or they require for the purposes of the preceding provisions of this Part of this Act.

15.—(1) Subject to such exceptions as may be prescribed—

(*a*) any term of a contract of a service (whenever made) or any rule of a personal or occupational pension scheme to the effect that an employed earner must be a member of a personal or occupational pension scheme, of a particular personal or occupational pension scheme or of one or other of a number of particular personal or occupational pension schemes shall be void; and

(*b*) any such term or rule to the effect that contributions shall be paid by or in respect of an employed earner to a particular personal or occupational pension scheme of which the earner is not a member, or to one or other of a number of personal or occupational pension schemes of none of which he is a member, shall be unenforceable for so long as he is not a member of the scheme or any of the schemes.

(2) Subsection (1) above shall not be construed so as to have the effect that an employer is required, when he would not otherwise be—

> (a) to make contributions to a personal or occupational pension scheme ; or
>
> (b) to increase an employed earner's pay in lieu of making contributions to a personal or occupational pension scheme.

Actuarial
tables.

16.—(1) Regulations prescribing actuarial tables for the purposes of any of the provisions to which this section applies—

> (a) shall be made only after consultation with the Government Actuary ; and
>
> (b) shall not be made unless a draft of them has been laid before Parliament and approved by a resolution of each House.

(2) This section applies—

1975 c. 60.

> (a) to sections 44, 44ZA, 44A and 45 of the Social Security Pensions Act 1975 ; and
>
> (b) to section 5 above.

(3) The tables—

> (a) shall embody whatever appears to the Secretary of State to be the best practical estimate of the average cost, expressed in actuarial terms and relative to a given period, of making such provision as is mentioned in section 44(5)(a) or (b), 44ZA(9)(b), 44A(3) or 45(2) of the Social Security Pensions Act 1975 or in section 5(10)(b) above, as the case may be ; and
>
> (b) shall assume for any period an average yield on investments which is not less than the average increase during that period in the general level of earnings obtaining in Great Britain,

but the regulations may provide for them to be adjusted according to whatever is from time to time the actual yield on prescribed investments or the average yield, as shown in prescribed published indices, on prescribed classes of investments.

(4) The Secretary of State may from time to time, and shall when required by subsection (6) below, lay before each House of Parliament—

> (a) a report by the Government Actuary on any changes in the factors affecting any of the actuarial tables prescribed for the purposes of any of the provisions to which this section applies (including changes affecting adjustments under the regulations) ; and

(*b*) a report by the Secretary of State stating whether he considers that the regulations ought to be altered in view of the Government Actuary's report and, if so, what alterations he proposes.

(5) The changes referred to in subsection (4)(*a*) above are, in the case of the first report under that paragraph, changes since the last report under section 46(3)(*a*) of the Social Security Pensions Act 1975 and, in the case of a subsequent report under this section, changes since the preparation of the last such report.

1975 c. 60

(6) The Secretary of State shall lay the first report under this section not later than 6th April 1987 and subsequent reports at intervals of not more than five years.

(7) If in a report under this section the Secretary of State proposes alterations in the regulations, he shall prepare and lay before each House of Parliament with the report draft regulations giving effect to the regulations and to be in force—

(*a*) from the beginning of such tax year as may be specified in the regulations not earlier than the second tax year after that in which the regulations are made ; or

(*b*) where it appears to him to be expedient for reasons of urgency, an earlier date not earlier than the date on which the regulations are made.

(8) If the draft regulations are approved by resolution of each House, the Secretary of State shall make the regulations in the form of the draft.

17.—(1) Regulations may provide that any provision which is contained in the Social Security Act 1973 or the Social Security Acts 1975 to 1986, other than a provision contained in this Part of this Act, and which relates to occupational pension schemes—

General power to modify statutory provisions.

1973 c. 38.

(*a*) shall have effect in relation to personal pension schemes subject to prescribed modifications ;

(*b*) shall have effect subject to such other modifications as the Secretary of State may consider necessary or expedient in consequence of this Part of this Act.

(2) Regulations may provide that any provision contained in an Act to which this subsection applies shall have effect subject to such modifications as the Secretary of State may consider necessary or expedient in consequence of this Part of this Act or in consequence of any corresponding enactment extending to Northern Ireland.

(3) The Acts to which subsection (2) above applies are—

(*a*) the Fire Services Act 1947 ;

1947 c. 41.

(*b*) the Sheriffs' Pensions (Scotland) Act 1961 ;

1961 c. 42.

PART I
1972 c. 11.
1972 c. 48.
1976 c. 35.
1978 c. 56.
1981 c. 20.

(c) the Superannuation Act 1972 ;

(d) the Parliamentary and other Pensions Act 1972 ;

(e) the Police Pensions Act 1976 ;

(f) the Parliamentary Pensions Act 1978 ;

(g) the Judicial Pensions Act 1981.

State earnings-related pension scheme

Additional
pensions.

18.—(1) In any enactment or instrument made under an enactment—

(a) a reference to a basic pension shall be substituted for any reference to the basic component of a long-term benefit ; and

(b) a reference to an additional pension shall be substituted for any reference to an additional component of such a benefit.

1975 c. 60.

(2) In subsection (2) of section 6 of the Social Security Pensions Act 1975 (rate of Category A retirement pension) the words " for a pensioner who attained pensionable age in a tax year before 6th April 1999 " shall be inserted before the word " shall ".

(3) The following subsections shall be inserted after that subsection—

" (2A) The additional pension for a pensioner who attained pensionable age in a tax year after 5th April 1999 shall be—

(a) in relation to any surpluses in the pensioner's earnings factors for the tax years in the period beginning with the tax year 1978-79 and ending with the tax year 1987-88, the weekly equivalent of $\dfrac{25}{N}$ per cent. of the amount of those surpluses ; and

(b) in relation to any surpluses in the pensioner's earnings factors in a tax year after the tax year 1987-88, the weekly equivalent of the relevant percentage of the amount of those surpluses ; and in this paragraph " relevant percentage " means—

(i) where the pensioner attained pensionable age in the tax year 2009-10 or any subsequent year, $\dfrac{20}{N}$;

(ii) where the pensioner attained pensionable age in a tax year falling within the period commencing with the tax year 1999-2000 and ending with the tax year 2008-2009, $\dfrac{20+X}{N}$.

(2B) In this section—

X=0·5 for each tax year by which the tax year in which the pensioner attained pensionable age precedes the tax year 2009-2010 ; and

N=the number of tax years in the pensioner's working life which fall after 5th April 1978 ;

and regulations may direct that in prescribed cases or classes of cases any tax year shall be disregarded for the purpose of calculating N, if it is a tax year after 5th April 1978 in which the pensioner—

(a) was credited with contributions or earnings under the principal Act by virtue of regulations under section 13(4) of that Act (credits to enable a person to satisfy contribution conditions) ; or

(b) was precluded from regular employment by responsibilities at home ; or

(c) in prescribed circumstances, would have been treated as falling within paragraph (a) or (b) above,

but not so as to reduce the number of years below 20.".

(4) In subsection (3) of that section, after " (2) " there shall be inserted " or (2A) ".

(5) For the purpose of determining the additional pension falling to be calculated under section 6 of the Social Security Pensions Act 1975 by virtue of section 7, 13 or 16(4) of that Act in a case where the deceased spouse died under pensionable age, the following definition shall be substituted for the definition of 1975 c. 60.

" N " in section 6(2B)—

" N=the number of tax years which begin after 5th April 1978 and end before the date when entitlement to the additional pension commences, except that where—

(a) in a case in which the deceased spouse was a man, that number would be greater than 49 ; or

(b) in a case in which the deceased spouse was a woman, that number would be greater than 44,

N=49 or 44, as the case may be ; ".

(6) For the purpose of determining the additional pension falling to be calculated under section 6 of that Act by virtue of section 14 of that Act (invalidity pension for persons under pensionable age), the following definition shall be substituted for the definition of " N " in section 6(2B)—

" N=the number of tax years which begin after 5th April 1978 and end before the first day of entitlement to the additional pension in the period of interruption of employment in which that day falls, except that where—

(*a*) in a case in which the person entitled to the pension is a man, that number would be greater than 49 ; or

(*b*) in a case in which the person so entitled is a woman, that number would be greater than 44,

N=49 or 44, as the case may be ;".

Additional pensions supplementary.
1975 c. 60.

19.—(1) The additional pension falling to be calculated under section 6 of the Social Security Pensions Act 1975 by virtue of any of the following provisions—

(*a*) section 7 (rate of widow's Category B retirement pension) ;

(*b*) section 8 (Category B retirement pension for widower) ;

(*c*) section 13 (rate of widowed mother's allowance and widow's pension) ; and

(*d*) section 16(4) (invalidity pension for widowers),

shall be one-half of the amount so calculated if the deceased spouse died after 5th April 2000.

(2) In paragraph 4 of Schedule 1 to that Act—

(*a*) the words " Subject to sub-paragraph (2A) below, where " shall be substituted for the word " Where ", in sub-paragraphs (1) and (2) ; and

(*b*) the following sub-paragraph shall be inserted after sub-paragraph (2)—

" (2A) If a married person dies after 5th April 2000, the rate of the retirement pension for that

person's widow or widower shall be increased by an
amount equivalent to the sum of—

(*a*) the increase in the basic pension to which the deceased spouse was entitled ; and

(*b*) one-half of the increase in the additional pension.".

(3) In sub-paragraph (1) of paragraph 4A of that Schedule after the word " increased " there shall be inserted the words " , subject to sub-paragraph (1A) below,".

(4) The following sub-paragraph shall be inserted after that sub-paragraph—

" (1A) Where the husband dies after 5th April 2000, sub-paragraph (1) above shall have effect in relation to his widow as if for the words from " the following amounts " onwards there were substituted the words " the following amounts—

(i) one-half of the appropriate amount after it has been reduced by the amount of any increases under section 37A of this Act ; and

(ii) one-half of any increase to which he had been entitled under this paragraph.".

(5) In sub-paragraph (2), after the word " increased " there shall be inserted the words " , subject to sub-paragraph (2A) below,".

(6) The following sub-paragraph shall be inserted after that sub-paragraph—

" (2A) Where the wife dies after 5th April 1989, sub-paragraph (2) above shall have effect as if for the words from " an amount ", in the first place where those words occur, to the end there were substituted—

(*a*) if she dies before 6th April 2000, the words " an amount equal to the sum of—

(i) that increase, so far as attributable to employment before 6th April 1988 ;

(ii) one-half of that increase, so far as attributable to employment after 5th April 1988 ;

(iii) the appropriate amount reduced by the amount of any increases under section 37A of this Act ; and

(iv) any increase to which she had been entitled under this paragraph." ; and

(b) if she dies after 5th April 2000, the words " an amount equal to the sum of—

(i) one-half of that increase so far as attributable to employment before 6th April 1988 ;

(ii) one-half of the appropriate amount after it has been reduced by the amount of any increases under section 37A of this Act ; and

(iii) one-half of any increase to which she had been entitled under this paragraph.".".

Part II

INCOME-RELATED BENEFITS

General

Income-related benefits.

20.—(1) Prescribed schemes shall provide for the following benefits (in this Act referred to as " income-related benefits ")—

(a) income support ;

(b) family credit ; and

(c) housing benefit.

(2) The Secretary of State shall make copies of schemes prescribed under subsection (1)(a) or (b) above available for public inspection at local offices of the Department of Health and Social Security at all reasonable hours without payment.

(3) A person in Great Britain is entitled to income support if—

(a) he is of or over the age of 16 ;

(b) he has no income or his income does not exceed the applicable amount ;

(c) he is not engaged in remunerative work and, if he is a member of a married or unmarried couple, the other member is not so engaged ; and (*d*) except in such circumstances as may be prescribed—

      (i) he is available for employment ;

      (ii) he is not receiving relevant education.

(4) Circumstances may be prescribed in which a person must not only satisfy the condition specified in subsection (3)(*d*)(i) above but also be registered in the prescribed manner for employment.

(5) Subject to regulations under section 51(1)(*a*) below, a person in Great Britain is entitled to family credit if, when the claim for it is made or is treated as made—

  (*a*) his income—

      (i) does not exceed the applicable amount ; or

      (ii) exceeds it, but only by such an amount that there is an amount remaining if the deduction for which section 21(3) below provides is made ;

  (*b*) he or, if he is a member of a married or unmarried couple, he or the other member of the couple, is engaged and normally engaged in remunerative work ; and

  (*c*) he or, if he is a member of a married or unmarried couple, he or the other member, is responsible for a member of the same household who is a child or a person of a prescribed description.

(6) Family credit shall be payable for a period of 26 weeks or such other period as may be prescribed, beginning with the week in which a claim for it is made or is treated as made and, subject to regulations, an award of family credit and the rate at which it is payable shall not be affected by any change of circumstances during that period.

(7) A person is entitled to housing benefit if—

  (*a*) he is liable to make payments in respect of a dwelling in Great Britain which he occupies as his home ;

  (*b*) there is an appropriate maximum housing benefit in his case ; and

  (*c*) either—

      (i) he has no income or his income does not exceed the applicable amount ; or

      (ii) his income exceeds that amount, but only by so much that there is an amount remaining if the deduction for which section 21(5) below provides is made.

(8) In subsection (7) above " payments in respect of a dwelling " means such payments as may be prescribed, but the power

to prescribe payments does not include power to prescribe mortgage payments or, in relation to Scotland, payments under heritable securities.

(9) Except in prescribed circumstances the entitlement of one member of a family to any one income-related benefit excludes entitlement to that benefit for any other member for the same period.

(10) Regulations may provide that an award of family credit shall terminate—

>   (*a*) if a person who was a member of the family at the date of the claim becomes a member of another family and some member of that family is entitled to family credit ; or

>   (*b*) if income support becomes payable in respect of a person who was a member of the family at the date of the claim for family credit.

(11) In this Part of this Act—

" child " means a person under the age of 16 ;

" family " means—

>   (*a*) a married or unmarried couple ;

>   (*b*) a married or unmarried couple and a member of the same household for whom one of them is or both are responsible and who is a child or a person of a prescribed description ;

>   (*c*) except in prescribed circumstances, a person who is not a member of a married or unmarried couple and a member of the same household for whom that person is responsible and who is a child or a person of a prescribed description ;

" married couple " means a man and woman who are married to each other and are members of the same household ;

" unmarried couple " means a man and woman who are not married to each other but are living together as husband and wife otherwise than in prescribed circumstances.

(12) Regulations may make provision for the purposes of this Part of this Act—

>   (*a*) as to circumstances in which a person is to be treated as being or not being in Great Britain ;

>   (*b*) continuing a person's entitlement to benefit during periods of temporary absence from Great Britain ;

>   (*c*) as to what is or is not to be treated as remunerative work or as employment ;

(*d*) as to circumstances in which a person is or is not to be treated as engaged or normally engaged in remunerative work or available for employment;   PART II

(*e*) as to what is or is not to be treated as relevant education;

(*f*) as to circumstances in which a person is or is not to be treated as receiving relevant education;

(*g*) as to circumstances in which a person is or is not to be treated as occupying a dwelling as his home;

(*h*) for treating any person who is liable to make payments in respect of a dwelling as if he were not so liable;

(*i*) for treating any person who is not liable to make payments in respect of a dwelling as if he were so liable;

(*j*) for treating as included in a dwelling any land used for the purposes of the dwelling;

(*k*) as to circumstances in which persons are to be treated as being or not being members of the same household;

(*l*) as to circumstances in which one person is to be treated as responsible or not responsible for another.

21.—(1) Where a person is entitled to income support—   Amount etc.

(*a*) if he has no income, the amount shall be the applicable amount; and

(*b*) if he has income, the amount shall be the difference between his income and the applicable amount.

(2) Where a person is entitled to family credit by virtue of section 20(5)(*a*)(i) above, the amount shall be the amount which is the appropriate maximum family credit in his case.

(3) Where a person is entitled to family credit by virtue of section 20(5)(*a*)(ii) above, the amount shall be what remains after the deduction from the appropriate maximum family credit of a prescribed percentage of the excess of his income over the applicable amount.

(4) Where a person is entitled to housing benefit by virtue of section 20(7)(*c*)(i) above, the amount shall be the amount which is the appropriate maximum housing benefit in his case.

(5) Where a person is entitled to housing benefit by virtue of section 20(7)(*c*)(ii) above, the amount shall be what remains after the deduction from the appropriate maximum housing benefit of prescribed percentages of the excess of his income over the applicable amount.

(6) Regulations shall prescribe the manner in which—

(*a*) the appropriate maximum family credit;

B 2

(*b*) the appropriate maximum housing benefit,
are to be determined in any case.

(7) Where the amount of any income-related benefit would be less than a prescribed amount, it shall not be payable except in prescribed circumstances.

Calculation.   **22.**—(1) The applicable amount shall be such amount or the aggregate of such amounts as may be prescribed.

(2) The power to prescribe applicable amounts conferred by subsection (1) above includes power to prescribe nil as an applicable amount.

(3) In relation to income support and housing benefit the applicable amount for a severely disabled person shall include an amount in respect of his being a severely disabled person.

(4) Regulations may specify circumstances in which persons are to be treated as being or as not being severely disabled.

(5) Where a person claiming an income-related benefit is a member of a family, the income and capital of any member of that family shall, except in prescribed circumstances, be treated as the income and capital of that person.

(6) No person shall be entitled to an income-related benefit if his capital or a prescribed part of it exceeds the prescribed amount.

(7) Regulations may provide that capital not exceeding the amount prescribed under subsection (6) above but exceeding a prescribed lower amount shall be treated, to a prescribed extent, as if it were income of a prescribed amount.

(8) Income and capital shall be calculated or estimated in such manner as may be prescribed.

(9) Circumstances may be prescribed in which—

(*a*) a person is treated as possessing capital or income which he does not possess ;

(*b*) capital or income which a person does possess is to be disregarded ;

(*c*) income is to be treated as capital ;

(*d*) capital is to be treated as income.

Income support

Trade
disputes.
1975 c. 14.   **23.**—(1) This section applies to a person, other than a child or a person of a prescribed description—

(*a*) who is disqualified under section 19 of the Social Security Act 1975 for receiving unemployment benefit ; or

(*b*) who would be so disqualified if otherwise entitled to that benefit, except during any period shown by the person to be a period of incapacity for work by reason of disease or bodily or mental disablement or to be within the maternity period.

(2) In subsection (1) above " the maternity period " means the period commencing at the beginning of the sixth week before the expected week of confinement and ending at the end of the seventh week after the week in which confinement takes place.

(3) For the purpose of calculating income support—

(*a*) so long as this section applies to a person who is not a member of a family, the applicable amount shall be disregarded ;

(*b*) so long as it applies to a person who is a member of a family but is not a member of a married or un-married couple, the portion of the applicable amount which is included in respect of him shall be disre-garded ;

(*c*) so long as it applies to one of the members of a married or unmarried couple—

(i) if the applicable amount consists only of an amount in respect of them, it shall be reduced to one-half ; and

(ii) if it includes other amounts, the portion of it which is included in respect of them shall be reduced to one-half and any further portion of it which is in-cluded in respect of the member of the couple to whom this section applies shall be disregarded ;

(*d*) so long as it applies to both the members of a married or unmarried couple—

(i) if neither of them is responsible for a child or person of a prescribed description who is a member of the same household, the applicable amount shall be disregarded ; and

(ii) in any other case, the portion of the applic-able amount which is included in respect of them and any further portion of it which is included in respect of either of them shall be disregarded.

(4) Where a reduction under subsection (3)(*c*) above would not produce a sum which is a multiple of 5p, the reduction shall be to the nearest lower sum which is such a multiple.

(5) Where this section applies to a person for any period, then, except so far as regulations provide otherwise—

(*a*) in calculating the entitlement to income support of that person or a member of his family the following shall be treated as his income and shall not be disregarded—

(i) any payment which he or a member of his

family receives or is entitled to obtain by reason of the person to whom this section applies being without employment for that period ; and

(ii) without prejudice to the generality of paragraph (i) above, any amount which becomes or would on an application duly made become available to him in that period by way of repayment of income tax deducted from his emoluments in pursuance of section 204 of the Income and Corporation Taxes Act 1970 ; and

(b) any payment by way of income support for that period or any part of it which apart from this paragraph would be made to him, or to a person whose applicable amount is aggregated with his—

(i) shall not be made if the weekly rate of payment is equal to or less than the relevant sum ; or

(ii) if it is more than the relevant sum, shall be at a weekly rate equal to the difference.

(6) In subsection (5) above " the relevant sum " means the amount which immediately before this section comes into force is specified in section 6(1)(b) of the Social Security (No. 2) Act 1980 increased by the percentage by which any order under section 63 below which brings alterations in the rates of benefits into force on the day on which this section comes into force increases the sums specified in subsection (3) of that section.

(7) If an order under section 63 below has the effect of increasing payments of income support, from the time when the order comes into force there shall be substituted, in subsection (5)(b) above, for the references to the sum for the time being mentioned in it references to a sum arrived at by—

(a) increasing that sum by the percentage by which applicable amounts have been increased by the order ; and

(b) if the sum as so increased is not a multiple of 50 pence, disregarding the remainder if it is 25 pence and, if it is not, rounding it up or down to the nearest 50 pence,

and the order shall state the substituted sum.

(8) If a person returns to work with the same employer after a period during which this section applies to him, then, until the end of the period of 15 days beginning with the day on which he returns to work with that employer, section 20(3) above shall have effect in relation to him as if the following paragraph were substituted for paragraph (c)—

" (c) he is a member of a married or unmarried couple and the other member is not engaged in remunerative work ; and " but any sum paid by way of income support for that period shall be recoverable in the prescribed manner from him or from any prescribed person.

24.—(1) Subject to the following provisions of this section, if income support is claimed by or in respect of a person whom another person is liable to maintain or paid to or in respect of such a person, the Secretary of State may make a complaint against the liable person to a magistrates' court for an order under this section.

(2) Except in a case falling within subsection (3) below, this section does not apply where the person who is liable to be maintained is an illegitimate child of the liable person.

(3) A case falls within this subsection if—

(a) the liable person is someone other than the child's father ; or

(b) the liable person is liable because he is a person such as is mentioned in section 26(3)(c) below.

(4) On the hearing of a complaint under this section the court shall have regard to all the circumstances and, in particular, to the income of the liable person, and may order him to pay such sum, weekly or otherwise, as it may consider appropriate, except that in a case falling within section 26(3)(c) below that sum shall not include any amount which is not attributable to income support (whether paid before or after the making of the order).

(5) In determining whether to order any payments to be made in respect of income support for any period before the complaint was made, or the amount of any such payments, the court shall disregard any amount by which the liable person's income exceeds the income which was his during that period.

(6) Any payments ordered to be made under this section shall be made—

(a) to the Secretary of State in so far as they are attributable to any income support (whether paid before or after the making of the order) ;

(b) to the person claiming income support or (if different) the dependant ; or

(c) to such other person as appears to the court expedient in the interests of the dependant.

(7) An order under this section shall be enforceable as an affiliation order.

(8) In the application of this section to Scotland, subsections (2), (3) and (7) shall be omitted and for the references to a

complaint and to a magistrates' court there shall be substituted respectively references to an application and to the sheriff.

(9) On an application under subsection (1) above a court in Scotland may make a finding as to the parentage of a child for the purpose of establishing whether a person is, for the purposes of this section and section 26 below, liable to maintain him.

Affiliation orders.

25.—(1) If—

  (a) income support is claimed by or in respect of an illegitimate child or paid in respect of such a child ; and

  (b) no affiliation order is in force ; and

  (c) the case does not fall within section 24(3) above,

the Secretary of State may, within three years from the time of the claim or payment, make application to a justice of the peace appointed for the commission area (within the meaning of the Justices of the Peace Act 1979) in which the mother of the child resides for a summons to be served under section 1 of the Affiliation Proceedings Act 1957.

1979 c. 55.

1957 c. 55.

(2) In any proceedings on an application under subsection (1) above the court shall hear such evidence as the Secretary of State may produce, and shall in all respects, subject to the provisions of subsection (3) below, proceed as on an application made by the mother under section 1 of the Affiliation Proceedings Act 1957.

(3) An affiliation order—

  (a) made on an application by the Secretary of State under subsection (1) above ; or

  (b) made on an application made by the Secretary of State in proceedings brought by the mother of the child under section 1 of the Affiliation Proceedings Act 1957,

may be made so as to provide that the payments or a part of the payments to be made under the order shall, instead of being made to a person entitled under section 5 of that Act, be made to the Secretary of State or to such other person as the court may direct.

(4) Any affiliation order, whether made before or after the commencement of this section, may, on the application of the Secretary of State, be varied so as to provide for the making of payments, or part of them, as mentioned in subsection (3) above ; and an application by the Secretary of State under this subsection may be made—

  (a) notwithstanding that the mother has died and no person has been appointed to have the custody of the child ; and

(*b*) where the child is not in the care of the mother and
she is not contributing to his maintenance, without
making her a party to the proceedings.

(5) An affiliation order which provides for the making of
payments, or part of them, as mentioned in subsection (3)
above, may, on the application of the mother of the child, be
varied so as to provide that the payments shall be made to a
person entitled under section 5 of the Affiliation Proceedings 1957 c. 55.
Act 1957.

26.—(1) If—

(*a*) any person persistently refuses or neglects to maintain
himself or any person whom he is liable to maintain;
and

(*b*) in consequence of his refusal or neglect income support
is paid to or in respect of him or such a person,

he shall be guilty of an offence and liable on summary conviction
to imprisonment for a term not exceeding three months or to a
fine of an amount not exceeding level 4 on the standard scale or
to both.

(2) For the purposes of subsection (1) above a person shall
not be taken to refuse or neglect to maintain himself or any
other person by reason only of anything done or omitted in
furtherance of a trade dispute.

(3) For the purposes of this section and sections 24 and 25
above—

(*a*) a man shall be liable to maintain his wife and his
children;

(*b*) a woman shall be liable to maintain her husband and
her children; and

(*c*) a person shall be liable to maintain another person
throughout any period in respect of which the first-
mentioned person has, on or after 23rd May 1980 (the
date of the passing of the Social Security Act 1980) 1980 c. 30.
and either alone or jointly with a further person, given
an undertaking in writing in pursuance of immigration
rules within the meaning of the Immigration Act 1971 1971 c. 77.
to be responsible for the maintenance and accommodation of the other person.

(4) In subsection (3) above—

(*a*) the reference to a man's children includes a reference
to children of whom he has been adjudged to be the
father; and

(*b*) the reference to a woman's children includes a reference
to her illegitimate children.

(5) Subsection (4) above does not apply to Scotland, and in the application of subsection (3) above to Scotland any reference to children shall be construed as a reference to children whether or not their parents have ever been married to one another.

(6) A document bearing a certificate which—

(a) is signed by a person authorised in that behalf by the Secretary of State ; and

(b) states that the document apart from the certificate is, or is a copy of, such an undertaking as is mentioned in subsection (3)(c) above,

shall be conclusive of the undertaking in question for the purpose of this section and section 24 above ; and a certificate purporting to be so signed shall be deemed to be so signed until the contrary is proved.

27.— (1) Where—

(a) a payment by way of prescribed income is made after the date which is the prescribed date in relation to the payment ; and

(b) it is determined that an amount which has been paid by way of income support would not have been paid if the payment had been made on the prescribed date,

the Secretary of State shall be entitled to recover that amount from the person to whom it was paid.

(2) Where—

(a) a prescribed payment which apart from this subsection falls to be made from public funds in the United Kingdom or under the law of any other member State is not made on or before the date which is the prescribed date in relation to the payment ; and

(b) it is determined that an amount (" the relevant amount ") has been paid by way of income support that would not have been paid if the payment mentioned in paragraph (a) above had been made on the prescribed date,

then—

(i) in the case of a payment from public funds in the United Kingdom, the authority responsible for making it may abate it by the relevant amount ; and

(ii) in the case of any other payment, the Secretary of State shall be entitled to receive the relevant amount out of the payment.

(3) Where—

(a) a person (in this subsection referred to as A) is entitled to any prescribed benefit for any period in respect of another person (in this subsection referred to as B) ; and

(*b*) either—

    (i) B has received income support for that period ; or

    (ii) B was, during that period, a member of the same family as some person other than A who received income support for that period ; and

(*c*) the amount of the income support has been determined on the basis that A has not made payments for the maintenance of B at a rate equal to or exceeding the amount of the prescribed benefit,

the amount of the prescribed benefit may, at the discretion of the authority administering it, be abated by the amount by which the amounts paid by way of income support exceed what it is determined that they would have been had A, at the time the amount of the income support was determined, been making payments for the maintenance of B at a rate equal to the amount of the prescribed benefit.

(4) Where an amount could have been recovered by abatement by virtue of subsection (2) or (3) above but has not been so recovered, the Secretary of State may recover it otherwise than by way of abatement—

(*a*) in the case of an amount which could have been recovered by virtue of subsection (2) above, from the person to whom it was paid ; and

(*b*) in the case of an amount which could have been recovered by virtue of subsection (3) above, from the person to whom the prescribed benefit in question was paid.

(5) Where a payment is made in a currency other than sterling, its value in sterling shall be determined for the purposes of this section in accordance with regulations.

Housing benefit

28.—(1) Housing benefit provided by virtue of a scheme under section 20(1) above (in this Act referred to as " the housing benefit scheme ")— Arrangements for housing benefit.

(*a*) is to be in the form of a rate rebate funded and administered by the appropriate rating authority, if it is in respect of payments by way of rates ;

(*b*) is to be in the form of a rent rebate funded and administered by the appropriate housing authority, if it is in respect of payments, other than payments by way of rates, to be made to a housing authority ; and

(c) is in any other case to be in the form of a rent allowance funded and administered by the appropriate local authority.

(2) Regulations may provide that in prescribed cases a payment made by a person entitled to a rent allowance shall be treated for the purposes of subsection (1)(a) above as being, to such extent as may be prescribed, a payment by way of rates.

(3) For the purposes of this section in its application to any dwelling—

(a) the appropriate rating authority is the rating authority for the area in which it is situated ;

(b) the appropriate housing authority is the housing authority to whom the occupier of the dwelling is liable to make payments ; and

(c) the appropriate local authority is the local authority for the area in which the dwelling is situated.

(4) Authorities may agree that one shall carry out responsibilities relating to housing benefit on another's behalf.

(5) Circumstances may be prescribed in which a rate rebate may be treated as if it fell to be paid as a rent allowance.

(6) An authority may modify any part of the housing benefit scheme administered by the authority—

(a) so as to provide for disregarding, in determining a person's income (whether he is the occupier of a dwelling or any other person whose income falls to be aggregated with that of the occupier of a dwelling), the whole or part of any war disablement pension or war widow's pension payable to that person ;

(b) to such extent in other respects as may be prescribed,

and any such modifications may be adopted by resolution of an authority.

(7) Modifications other than such modifications as are mentioned in subsection (6)(a) above shall be so framed as to secure that, in the estimate of the authority adopting them, the total of the rebates or allowances which will be granted by the authority in any year will not exceed the permitted total of rebates or allowances for that year.

(8) An authority who have adopted modifications may by resolution revoke or vary them.

(9) If the housing benefit scheme includes power for an authority to exercise a discretion in awarding housing benefit, the authority shall not exercise that discretion so that the total of the rebates or allowances granted by them in any year

exceeds the permitted total of rebates or allowances for that year.

(10) In relation to any authority the permitted total of rebates or allowances for any year shall be calculated, in the manner specified by an order made by the Secretary of State, by reference to the total housing benefit granted by that authority during the year, less such deductions as are specified in the order.

29.—(1) Regulations shall require authorities to notify a person who has claimed housing benefit of their determination of that claim.

(2) Any such notification shall be given in such form as may be prescribed.

(3) Regulations shall make provision for reviews of determinations relating to housing benefit.

(4) Except where regulations otherwise provide, any amount of housing benefit paid in excess of entitlement may be recovered in such manner as may be prescribed either by the Secretary of State or by the authority which paid the benefit.

(5) Regulations may require such an authority to recover such an amount in such circumstances as may be prescribed.

(6) An amount recoverable under this section is in all cases recoverable from the person to whom it was paid; but, in such circumstances as may be prescribed, it may also be recovered from such other person as may be prescribed.

(7) Any amount recoverable under this section may, without prejudice to any other method of recovery, be recovered by deduction from prescribed benefits.

30.—(1) For each year the Secretary of State shall pay—

   (*a*) a subsidy to be known as " rate rebate subsidy " to each rating authority;

   (*b*) a subsidy to be known as " rent rebate subsidy " to each housing authority; and

   (*c*) a subsidy to be known as " rent allowance subsidy " to each local authority.

(2) The subsidy under subsection (1) above which is to be paid to an authority—

   (*a*) shall be calculated, in the manner specified by an order made by the Secretary of State, by reference to the total housing benefit granted by that authority during the year with any additions specified in the order but subject to any deductions so specified ; and

(b) shall be subject to deduction of any amount which the Secretary of State considers it unreasonable to meet out of money provided by way of subsidy under subsection (1) above.

(3) For each year the Secretary of State may pay to an authority as part of the subsidy under subsection (1) above an additional sum calculated, in the manner specified by an order made by the Secretary of State, in respect of the costs of administering housing benefit.

(4) The Secretary of State may pay to an authority, for the financial year 1987-88, a subsidy, calculated in the manner specified by an order made by the Secretary of State, in connection with the costs incurred by the authority in implementing the housing benefit scheme.

(5) Rent rebate subsidy shall be payable—

(a) in the case of a local authority in England and Wales—

(i) for the credit of their Housing Revenue Account to the extent that it is calculated by reference to Housing Revenue Account rebates and any costs of administering such rebates ; and

(ii) for the credit of their general rate fund to the extent that it is not so calculated ;

(b) in the case of a local authority in Scotland, for the credit of their rent rebate account ;

(c) in the case of a new town corporation in England and Wales or the Development Board for Rural Wales, for the credit of their housing account ; and

(d) in the case of a new town corporation in Scotland or the Scottish Special Housing Association, for the credit of the account to which rent rebates granted by them are debited.

(6) Every local authority shall make for each year a rate fund contribution to their Housing Revenue Account of an amount equal to the difference between—

(a) so much of their rent rebate subsidy for the year as is credited to that Account ; and

(b) the total of—

(i) the Housing Revenue Account rebates granted by them during the year ; and

(ii) the cost of administering such rebates.

(7) Rent allowance subsidy shall be payable—

(a) in the case of a local authority in England and Wales, for the credit of their general rate fund ; and

(*b*) in the case of a local authority in Scotland, for the credit
    of their rent allowance account.

(8) Subsidy under this section shall be payable by the Secretary
of State at such time and in such manner as the Treasury may
direct, but subject—

(*a*) to the making of a claim for it in such form and con-
    taining such particulars as the Secretary of State may
    from time to time determine ; and

(*b*) to such conditions as to records, certificates, audit
    or otherwise as the Secretary of State may, with the
    approval of the Treasury, impose.

(9) The amount of any subsidy payable to an authority shall
be calculated to the nearest pound, by disregarding an odd
amount of 50 pence or less and by treating an odd amount
exceeding 50 pence as a whole pound.

(10) If an order made by the Secretary of State so provides—

(*a*) the rate fund contribution under subsection (6) above
    made by a local authority for any year ; and

(*b*) the rent allowances granted by a local authority during
    any year,

or such proportion of them as may be calculated in the manner
specified by the order, shall not count as relevant expenditure
for the purposes of section 54 of the Local Government, Planning 1980 c. 65.
and Land Act 1980 (rate support grant).

31.—(1) The Secretary of State may supply to authorities such Information.
information of a prescribed description obtained by reason of
the exercise of any of his functions under the benefit Acts as they
may require in connection with any of their functions relating
to housing benefit.

(2) Authorities shall supply to the Secretary of State such information of a prescribed description obtained by reason of the
exercise of their functions relating to housing benefit as he may
require in connection with any of his functions under the benefit
Acts.

(3) It shall also be the duty of an authority to supply the
Secretary of State, in the prescribed manner and within the prescribed time—

(*a*) with such information as he may require concerning
    their performance of any of their functions relating to
    housing benefit ; and

(*b*) with such information as he may require to enable
    him—

        (i) to prepare estimates of likely future amounts of
        housing benefit expenditure ; and

(ii) to decide questions relating to the development of housing benefit policy.

(4) Every authority granting housing benefit—

    (*a*) shall take such steps as appear to them appropriate for the purpose of securing that persons who may be entitled to housing benefit from the authority become aware that they may be entitled to it ; and

    (*b*) shall make copies of the housing benefit scheme, with any modifications adopted by them under section 28 above, available for public inspection at their principal office at all reasonable hours without payment.

(5) In order to assist authorities to give effect to the housing benefit scheme, where a rent is registered under Part IV of the Rent Act 1977, there shall be noted on the register the amount (if any) of the registered rent which, in the opinion of the rent officer or rent assessment committee, is fairly attributable to the provision of services, except any amount which is negligible in the opinion of the officer or, as the case may be, the committee.

1977 c. 42.

PART III

THE SOCIAL FUND

The social
fund and
social fund
officers.

32.—(1) There shall be established a fund, to be known as the social fund.

(2) Payments may be made out of that fund, in accordance with this Part of this Act—

    (*a*) to meet, in prescribed circumstances, maternity expenses and funeral expenses ; and

    (*b*) to meet other needs in accordance with directions given or guidance issued by the Secretary of State.

(3) Payments under this section shall be known as " social fund payments ".

(4) Social fund payments to meet funeral expenses may in all cases be recovered, as if they were funeral expenses, out of the estate of the deceased, and (subject to section 53 below) by no other means.

(5) The social fund shall be maintained under the control and management of the Secretary of State and payments out of it shall be made by him.

(6) The Secretary of State shall make payments into the social fund of such amounts, at such times and in such manner as he may with the approval of the Treasury determine.

(7) Accounts of the social fund shall be prepared in such form, and in such manner and at such times, as the Treasury may

direct, and the Comptroller and Auditor General shall examine
and certify every such account and shall lay copies of it, together
with his report, before Parliament.

(8) The Secretary of State shall appoint officers, to be known as
" social fund officers ", for the purpose of performing functions
in relation to social fund payments such as are mentioned in
subsection (2)(b) above ; and the Secretary of State may allocate
an amount, or allocate different amounts for different purposes,
for such payments by a particular social fund officer or group of
officers in a financial year.

(9) A social fund officer may be appointed to perform all the
functions of social fund officers or such functions of such officers
as may be specified in his instrument of appointment.

33.—(1) A social fund payment such as is mentioned in section Awards by
32(2)(b) above may be awarded to a person only if an application social fund
for such a payment has been made by him or on his behalf. officers.

(2) The questions whether such a payment is to be awarded
and how much it is to be shall be determined by a social fund
officer.

(3) A social fund officer may determine that an award shall be
payable in specified instalments at specified times.

(4) A social fund officer may determine that an award is to
be repayable.

(5) An award which is repayable shall be recoverable by the
Secretary of State.

(6) Without prejudice to any other method of recovery, the
Secretary of State may recover an award by deduction from
prescribed benefits.

(7) The Secretary of State may recover an award—
  (a) from the person to or for the benefit of whom it was
      made ;
  (b) where that person is a member of a married or un-
      married couple, from the other member of the couple ;
  (c) from a person who is liable to maintain the person by
      or on behalf of whom the application for the award was
      made or any person in relation to whose needs the
      award was made.

(8) Subsections (3) to (6) of section 26 above have effect for
the purposes of subsection (7)(c) above as they have effect for
the purposes of sections 24 to 26 above.

(9) In determining whether to make an award to the applicant
or the amount or value to be awarded an officer shall have regard,

subject to subsection (10) below, to all the circumstances of the case and, in particular—

 (*a*) the nature, extent and urgency of the need ;

 (*b*) the existence of resources from which the need may be met ;

 (*c*) the possibility that some other person or body may wholly or partly meet it ;

 (*d*) where the payment is repayable, the likelihood of repayment and the time within which repayment is likely ;

 (*e*) any relevant allocation under section 32(8) above.

(10) An officer shall determine any question under this section in accordance with any general directions issued by the Secretary of State and in determining any such question shall take account of any general guidance issued by him.

(11) Payment of an award shall be made to the applicant unless the social fund officer determines otherwise.

(12) In this section " married couple " and " unmarried couple " are to be construed in accordance with Part II of this Act and regulations made under it.

Reviews.

34.—(1) A social fund officer—

 (*a*) shall review a determination made under this Part of this Act by himself or some other social fund officer, if an application for a review is made to him within such time and in such form and manner as may be prescribed by or on behalf of the person who applied for the social fund payment to which the determination relates ; and

 (*b*) may review such a determination in such other circumstances as he thinks fit ;

and may exercise on a review any power exercisable by an officer under section 33 above.

(2) The power to review a determination conferred on a social fund officer by subsection (1) above includes power to review a determination made by a social fund officer on a previous review.

(3) On an application made by or on behalf of the person to whom a determination relates within such time and in such form and manner as may be prescribed a determination of a social fund officer which has been reviewed shall be further reviewed by a social fund inspector appointed by the social fund Commissioner under section 35 below.

(4) On a review a social fund inspector shall have the following powers—

 (*a*) power to confirm the determination made by the social fund officer ;

(b) power to make any determination which a social fund
   officer could have made ;

(c) power to refer the matter to a social fund officer for
   determination.

(5) A social fund inspector may review a determination under
subsection (3) above made by himself or some other social fund
inspector.

(6) In determining a question on a review a social fund officer
or social fund inspector shall have regard, subject to subsection
(7) below, to all the circumstances of the case and, in particular,
to the matters specified in section 33(9)(a) to (e) above.

(7) An officer or inspector shall determine any question on a
review in accordance with any general directions issued by the
Secretary of State under section 33(10) above and any general
directions issued by him with regard to reviews and in determining any such question shall take account of any general
guidance issued by him under that subsection or with regard to
reviews.

(8) Directions under this section may specify—

(a) the circumstances in which a determination is to be
   reviewed ; and

(b) the manner in which a review is to be conducted.

35.—(1) There shall be an officer to be known as the social The social
fund Commissioner (in this section referred to as " the Com- fund
missioner "). Commissioner.

(2) The Commissioner shall be appointed by the Secretary of
State.

(3) The Commissioner—

(a) shall appoint such social fund inspectors ;

(b) may appoint such officers and staff for himself and for
   social fund inspectors, as he thinks fit, but with the
   consent of the Secretary of State and the Treasury as to
   numbers.

(4) Appointments under subsection (3) above shall be made
from persons made available to the Commissioner by the Secretary of State.

(5) It shall be the duty of the Commissioner—

(a) to monitor the quality of decisions of social fund inspectors and give them such advice and assistance as he
   thinks fit to improve the standard of their decisions ;

(b) to arrange such training of social fund inspectors as he
   considers appropriate ; and

PART III

(*c*) to carry out such other functions in connection with the work of social fund inspectors as the Secretary of State may direct.

(6) The Commissioner shall report annually in writing to the Secretary of State on the standards of reviews by social fund inspectors and the Secretary of State shall publish his report.

PART IV

BENEFITS UNDER SOCIAL SECURITY ACT 1975

Widowhood.
1975 c. 14.

36.—(1) The following section shall be substituted for section 24 of the Social Security Act 1975—

"Widow's payment.

24.—(1) Subject to subsection (2) below, a woman who has been widowed shall be entitled to a widow's payment of the amount specified in relation thereto in Schedule 4, Part IA, if—

(*a*) she was under pensionable age at the time when her late husband died, or he was then not entitled to a Category A retirement pension (section 28) ; and

(*b*) her late husband satisfied the contribution condition for a widow's payment specified in Schedule 3, Part I, paragraph 4.

(2) The payment shall not be payable to a widow if she and a man to whom she is not married are living together as husband and wife at the time of her husband's death.".

(2) The following shall be inserted after Part I of Schedule 4 to that Act—

" PART IA

WIDOW'S PAYMENT

Widow's payment (section 24).		£1,000·00.".

(3) In section 26—

(*a*) in subsection (1), for " 40 ", where occurring in paragraphs (*a*) and (*b*), there shall be substituted " 45 " ; and

(*b*) in subsection (2), for " 50 ", in both places where it occurs, there shall be substituted " 55 ".

Invalid care
allowance for
women.

37.—(1) Section 37(3) of the Social Security Act 1975 shall have effect, and shall be treated as having had effect from 22nd December 1984, as if the words from " and a woman " to the end were omitted.

(2) The Social Security Benefit (Dependency) Regulations PART IV
1977 shall have effect, and shall be treated as having had effect S.I. 1977/343.
from 22nd December 1984, as if the following sub-paragraphs
were substituted for sub-paragraphs (a) and (b) of paragraph 7
of Schedule 2 (increases of invalid care allowance)—

" (a) a spouse who is not engaged in any one or more employments from which the spouse's weekly earnings
exceed that amount ; or

(b) some person (not being a child) who—

(i) has the care of a child or children in respect
of whom the beneficiary is entitled to child benefit,
being a child or children in respect of whom the
beneficiary is entitled to an increase of an invalid
care allowance or would be so entitled but for the
provisions of any regulations for the time being in
force under the Act relating to overlapping benefits ;

(ii) is not undergoing imprisonment or detention
in legal custody ;

(iii) is not engaged in any one or more employments (other than employment by the beneficiary
in caring for a child or children in respect of whom
the beneficiary is entitled to child benefit) from
which the person's weekly earnings exceed that
amount ;

(iv) is not absent from Great Britain, except for
any period during which the person is residing with
the beneficiary outside Great Britain and for which
the beneficiary is entitled to an invalid care allowance.".

38.—(1) The provisions to which this subsection applies shall Abolition of
cease to have effect. maternity
grant.

(2) The provisions to which subsection (1) above applies are—

(a) in the Social Security Act 1975— 1975 c. 14.

(i) section 21 ; and

(ii) Schedule 4, Part II, paragraph 1 ; and

(b) section 5 of the Social Security Act 1980. 1980 c. 30.

(3) If a woman is confined after the commencement of subsection (1) above, she shall nevertheless be entitled to maternity
grant if—

(a) her expected date of confinement was before the commencement of that subsection ; and

(b) she has claimed the grant before the date of her confinement.

PART IV
1975 c. 14.

(4) No regulations made under section 21(5) of the Social Security Act 1975 shall apply to a woman whose expected date of confinement is after the commencement of subsection (1) above.

Industrial
injuries and
diseases.

39. Schedule 3 to this Act shall have effect in relation to Chapters IV and V of Part II of the Social Security Act 1975 and associated enactments.

Abolition of
child's special
allowance
except for
existing
beneficiaries.

40. A child's special allowance under section 31 of the Social Security Act 1975 shall not be payable for any period after this section comes into force except to a beneficiary who—

   (*a*) immediately before the date on which this section comes into force satisfied the conditions for entitlement set out in paragraphs (*a*) to (*c*) of that section and was not barred from payment of the allowance by the proviso to it ; and

   (*b*) has so continued since that date.

Abolition of
death grant.

41. Death grant shall not be payable in respect of a death which occurs after the commencement of this section.

Abolition of
reduced rate
of short-term
benefits.

42. Paragraphs (*a*) to (*c*) of section 33(1) of the Social Security Act 1975 (reduced rate of short-term benefits payable on partial satisfaction of contribution conditions) shall cease to have effect.

Unemploy-
ment benefit—
disqualifica-
tion.

43.—(1) The following subsection shall be substituted for section 18(4) of the Social Security Act 1975—

   " (4) Regulations may provide for a person who would be entitled to unemployment benefit but for the operation of any provision of this Act or of regulations disentitling him to it or disqualifying him for it to be treated as if entitled to it for the purposes of this section.".

(2) " 13 " shall be substituted for " 6 "—

   (*a*) in section 20(1) of that Act ; and

S.I. 1983/1399.

   (*b*) in regulation 8(4)(*b*) of the Supplementary Benefit (Requirements) Regulations 1983.

(3) In the Social Security Act 1975—

   (*a*) the following subsection shall be inserted after section 20(1)—

     " (1A) The Secretary of State may by order substitute a longer or shorter period for the period for the time being mentioned in subsection (1) above." ; and

   (*b*) in section 167(1)(*b*) (affirmative procedure for certain orders) the words " section 20(1A) " shall be inserted

before the word " or ", in the second place where it
occurs.

44.—(1) The following subsections shall be substituted for
subsection (1) of section 19 of the Social Security Act 1975
(disqualification for unemployment benefit)—

" (1) Subject to the following provisions of this section—

    (*a*) an employed earner who has lost employment as an employed earner by reason of a stoppage of work due to a trade dispute at his place of employment is disqualified for receiving unemployment benefit for any day during the stoppage unless he proves that he is not directly interested in the dispute ; and

    (*b*) an employed earner who has withdrawn his labour in furtherance of a trade dispute but does not fall within paragraph (*a*) above is disqualified for receiving unemployment benefit for any day on which his labour remains withdrawn.

(1A) A person disqualified under subsection (1)(*a*) above for receiving unemployment benefit shall cease to be so disqualified if he proves that during the stoppage—

    (*a*) he has become bona fide employed elsewhere ; or

    (*b*) his employment has been terminated by reason of redundancy within the meaning of section 81(2) of the Employment Protection (Consolidation) Act 1978 ; or

    (*c*) he has bona fide resumed employment with his employer but has subsequently left for a reason other than the trade dispute.".

(2) The following shall be inserted after section 49 of that Act—

" Trade disputes

49A. A beneficiary shall not be entitled—

    (*a*) to an increase in any benefit under sections 44 to 48 above ; or

    (*b*) to an increase in benefit for an adult dependant by virtue of regulations under section 49 above,

if the person in respect of whom he would be entitled to the increase—

    (i) is disqualified under section 19 above for receiving unemployment benefit ; or

               (ii) would be so disqualified if he were otherwise entitled to that benefit.".

Guardian's
allowance—
adoption.
1975 c. 14.

45. In section 38 of the Social Security Act 1975 (guardian's allowance)—

    (a) in subsection (6), for the word " No " there shall be substituted the words " Subject to subsection (7) below, no " ; and

    (b) the following subsection shall be inserted after subsection (6)—

        " (7) Where a person—

           (a) has adopted a child ; and

           (b) was entitled to guardian's allowance in respect of the child immediately before the adoption,

      subsecton (6) above shall not terminate his entitlement.".

PART V

MATERNITY PAY ETC.

Statutory
maternity
pay—
entitlement
and liability
to pay.

46.—(1) Subject to the following provisions of this Act, where a woman who is or has been an employee satisfies the conditions set out in this section, she shall be entitled to payments to be known as " statutory maternity pay ".

    (2) The conditions mentioned in subsection (1) above are—

    (a) that she has been in employed earner's employment with an employer for a continuous period of at least 26 weeks ending with the week immediately preceding the 14th week before the expected week of confinement but has ceased to work for him, wholly or partly because of pregnancy or confinement ;

    (b) that her normal weekly earnings for the period of 8 weeks ending with the week immediately preceding the 14th week before the expected week of confinement are not less than the lower earnings limit in force under section 4(1)(a) of the Social Security Act 1975 immediately before the commencement of the 14th week before the expected week of confinement ; and

    (c) that she has become pregnant and has reached, or been confined before reaching, the commencement of the 11th week before the expected week of confinement.

    (3) The liability to make payments of statutory maternity pay to a woman is a liability of any person of whom she has been an employee as mentioned in subsection (2)(a) above.

(4) Except in such cases as may be prescribed, a woman shall   PART V
be entitled to payments of statutory maternity pay only if—

    (*a*) she gives the person who will be liable to pay it notice
that she is going to be absent from work with him,
wholly or partly because of pregnancy or confinement ;
and

    (*b*) the notice is given at least 21 days before her absence
from work is due to begin or, if that is not reasonably
practicable, as soon as is reasonably practicable.

(5) The notice shall be in writing if the person who is liable
to pay the woman statutory maternity pay so requests.

(6) Any agreement shall be void to the extent that it purports—

    (*a*) to exclude, limit or otherwise modify any provision of
this Part of this Act ; or

    (*b*) to require an employee or former employee to contri-
bute (whether directly or indirectly) towards any costs
incurred by her employer or former employer under
this Part of this Act ;

but section 23A of the Social Security and Housing Benefits 1982 c. 24.
Act 1982 shall have effect in relation to paragraph (*a*) above as
it has effect in relation to section 1(2)(*a*) of that Act but as if the
reference to statutory sick pay were a reference to statutory
maternity pay.

(7) Regulations shall make provision as to a former employer's liability to pay statutory maternity pay to a woman in any
case where the former employer's contract of service with her
has been brought to an end by the former employer solely, or
mainly, for the purpose of avoiding liability for statutory maternity pay.

(8) The Secretary of State may by regulations—

    (*a*) specify circumstances in which, notwithstanding the
foregoing provisions of this section, there is to be no
liability to pay statutory maternity pay in respect of
a week ;

    (*b*) specify circumstances in which, notwithstanding the fore-
going provisions of this section, the liability to make
payments of statutory maternity pay is to be a liability
of his ;

    (*c*) specify in what circumstances employment is to be
treated as continuous for the purposes of this Part of
this Act ;

    (*d*) provide that a woman is to be treated as being em-
ployed for a continuous period of at least 26 weeks
where—

        (i) she has been employed by the same employer

for at least 26 weeks under 2 or more separate contracts of service ; and

(ii) those contracts were not continuous ;

(e) provide that subsection (2)(a) or (b) above or both
shall have effect subject to prescribed modifications—

(i) where a woman has been dismissed from her
employment ;

(ii) where a woman is confined before the beginning of the 14th week before the expected week of
confinement ; and

(iii) in such other cases as may be prescribed ;

(f) provide for amounts earned by a woman under separate contracts of service with the same employer to
be aggregated for the purposes of this Part of this
Act ; and

(g) provide that the amount of a woman's earnings for
any period, or the amount of her earnings to be
treated as comprised in any payment made to her or
for her benefit, shall be calculated or estimated in such
manner and on such basis as may be prescribed and
that for that purpose payments of a particular class
or description made or falling to be made to or by a
woman shall, to such extent as may be prescribed,
be disregarded or, as the case may be, be deducted
from the amount of her earnings.

The maternity
pay period.

47.—(1) Subject to the provisions of this Part of this Act,
statutory maternity pay shall be payable in respect of each
week during a prescribed period (" the maternity pay period ")
of a duration not exceeding 18 weeks.

(2) Subject to subsections (3) and (7) below, the first week
of the maternity pay period shall be the 11th week before the
expected week of confinement.

(3) Cases may be prescribed in which the first week of the
period is to be a prescribed week later than the 11th week
before the expected week of confinement, but not later than
the 6th week before the expected week of confinement.

(4) Statutory maternity pay shall not be payable to a woman
by a person in respect of any week during any part of which
she works under a contract of service with him.

(5) It is immaterial for the purposes of subsection (4) above
whether the work referred to in that paragraph is work under
a contract of service which existed immediately before the
maternity pay period or a contract of service which did not so
exist.

(6) Except in such cases as may be prescribed, statutory maternity pay shall not be payable to a woman in respect of any week after she has been confined and during any part of which she works for any employer who is not liable to pay her statutory maternity pay.

(7) Regulations may provide that this section shall have effect subject to prescribed modifications in relation—

(*a*) to cases in which a woman has been confined before the 11th week before the expected week of confinement ; and

(*b*) to cases in which—

(i) a woman is confined between the 11th and 6th weeks before the expected week of confinement ; and

(ii) the maternity pay period has not then commenced for her.

48.—(1) There shall be two rates of statutory maternity pay, in this Act referred to as " the higher rate " and " the lower rate ".

(2) The higher rate is a weekly rate equivalent to nine-tenths of a woman's normal weekly earnings for the period of 8 weeks immediately preceding the 14th week before the expected week of confinement.

(3) The lower rate is such weekly rate as may be prescribed.

(4) Subject to the following provisions of this section, statutory maternity pay shall be payable at the higher rate to a woman who for a continuous period of at least 2 years ending with the week immediately preceding the 14th week before the expected week of confinement has been an employee in employed earner's employment of any person liable to pay it to her, and shall be so paid by any such person in respect of the first 6 weeks in respect of which it is payable.

(5) Statutory maternity pay shall not be payable at the higher rate to a woman whose relations with the person liable to pay it are or were governed by a contract of service which normally involves or involved employment for less than 16 hours weekly unless during a continuous period of at least 5 years ending with the week immediately preceding the 14th week before the expected week of confinement her contract of service normally involved employment for 8 hours or more weekly.

(6) The Secretary of State may by regulations make provision as to when a contract of service is to be treated for the purposes of subsection (5) above as normally involving or having involved employment—

(*a*) for less than 16 hours weekly ; or

PART V   (*b*) for 8 hours or more weekly,

or as not normally involving or having involved such employment.

(7) Statutory maternity pay shall be payable to a woman at the lower rate if she is entitled to statutory maternity pay but is not entitled to payment at the higher rate.

(8) If a woman is entitled to statutory maternity pay at the higher rate, she shall be entitled to it at the lower rate in respect of the portion of the maternity pay period after the end of the 6 week period mentioned in subsection (4) above.

Further provisions relating to statutory maternity pay etc.

1975 c. 14.
1978 c. 44.

49.—(1) Part I of Schedule 4 to this Act shall have effect for supplementing this Part of this Act.

(2) The Social Security Act 1975 shall have effect subject to the amendments set out in Part II of that Schedule.

(3) Part III of that Schedule shall have effect in relation to maternity pay under the Employment Protection (Consolidation) Act 1978 and to the Maternity Pay Fund.

Interpretation of Part V.

50.—(1) In this Part of this Act (including Schedule 4 to this Act)—

" confinement " means labour resulting in the issue of a living child, or labour after 28 weeks of pregnancy resulting in the issue of a child whether alive or dead, and " confined " shall be construed accordingly ; and where a woman's labour begun on one day results in the issue of a child on another day she shall be taken to be confined on the day of the issue of the child or, if labour results in the issue of twins or a greater number of children, she shall be taken to be confined on the day of the issue of the last of them ;

" dismissed " is to be construed in accordance with section 55(2) to (7) of the Employment Protection (Consolidation) Act 1978 ;

" employee " means a woman who is—

(*a*) gainfully employed in Great Britain either under a contract of service or in an office (including elective office) with emoluments chargeable to income tax under Schedule E ; and

(*b*) over the age of 16 ;

but subject to regulations which may provide for cases where any such woman is not to be treated as an employee for the purposes of this Part of this Act and for cases where a woman who would not otherwise be an employee for those purposes is to be treated as an employee for those purposes ;

" employer ", in relation to a woman who is an employee and a contract of service of hers, means a person who under section 4 of the Social Security Act 1975 is, or but for subsection (2)(*b*) of that section would be, liable to pay secondary Class 1 contributions in relation to any of her earnings (within the meaning of that Act) under the contract ;

" maternity pay period " has the meaning assigned to it by section 47(1) above ;

" week " means a period of 7 days beginning with midnight between Saturday and Sunday or such other period as may be prescribed in relation to any particular case or class of cases.

(2) Without prejudice to any other power to make regulations under this Part of this Act, regulations may specify cases in which, for the purposes of this Part of this Act or of such provisions of this Part of this Act as may be prescribed—

(*a*) two or more employers are to be treated as one ;

(*b*) two or more contracts of service in respect of which the same woman is an employee are to be treated as one.

(3) For the purposes of this Part of this Act a woman's normal weekly earnings shall, subject to subsection (5) below, be taken to be the average weekly earnings which in the relevant period have been paid to her or paid for her benefit under the contract of service with the employer in question.

(4) For the purposes of subsection (3) above " earnings " and " relevant period " shall have the meanings given to them by regulations.

(5) In such cases as may be prescribed a woman's normal weekly earnings shall be calculated in accordance with regulations.

PART VI

COMMON PROVISIONS

Administration

51.—(1) Regulations may provide—

(*a*) for requiring a claim for a benefit to which this section applies to be made by such person, in such manner and within such time as may be prescribed ;

(*b*) for treating such a claim made in such circumstances as may be prescribed as having been made at such date earlier or later than that at which it is made as may be prescribed ;

(c) for permitting such a claim to be made, or treated as if made, for a period wholly or partly after the date on which it is made ;

(d) for permitting an award on such a claim to be made for such a period subject to the condition that the claimant satisfies the requirements for entitlement when benefit becomes payable under the award ;

(e) for a review of any such award if those requirements are found not to have been satisfied ;

(f) for the disallowance on any ground of a person's claim for a benefit to which this section applies to be treated as a disallowance of any further claim by that person for that benefit until the grounds of the original disallowance have ceased to exist ;

(g) for enabling one person to act for another in relation to a claim for a benefit to which this section applies and for enabling such a claim to be made and proceeded with in the name of a person who has died ;

(h) for requiring any information or evidence needed for the determination of such a claim or of any question arising in connection with such a claim to be furnished by such person as may be prescribed in accordance with the regulations ;

(j) for a claim for any one benefit to which this section applies to be treated, either in the alternative or in addition, as a claim for any other such benefit that may be prescribed ;

(k) for the person to whom, time when and manner in which a benefit to which this section applies is to be paid and for the information and evidence to be furnished in connection with the payment of such a benefit ;

(l) for notice to be given of any change of circumstances affecting the continuance of entitlement to such a benefit or payment of such a benefit ;

(m) for the day on which entitlement to such a benefit is to begin or end ;

(n) for calculating the amounts of such a benefit according to a prescribed scale or otherwise adjusting them so as to avoid fractional amounts or facilitate computation ;

(o) for extinguishing the right to payment of such a benefit if payment is not obtained within such period, not being less than 12 months, as may be prescribed from

the date on which the right is treated under the regula- PART VI
tions as having arisen ;

(*p*) for suspending payment, in whole or in part, where it
appears to the Secretary of State that a question arises
whether—

(i) the conditions for entitlement are or were ful-
filled ;

(ii) an award ought to be revised ;

(iii) an appeal ought to be brought against an
award ;

(*q*) for withholding payments of a benefit to which this
section applies in prescribed circumstances and for
subsequently making withheld payments in prescribed
circumstances ;

(*r*) for the circumstances and manner in which payments of
such a benefit may be made to another person on
behalf of the beneficiary for any purpose, which may
be to discharge, in whole or in part, an obligation of
the beneficiary or any other person ;

(*s*) for the payment or distribution of such a benefit to or
among persons claiming to be entitled on the death of
any person and for dispensing with strict proof of their
title ;

(*t*) for the making of a payment on account of such a
benefit—

(i) where no claim has been made and it is im-
practicable for one to be made immediately ;

(ii) where a claim has been made and it is im-
practicable for the claim or an appeal, reference,
review or application relating to it to be immediately
determined ;

(iii) where an award has been made but it is im-
practicable to pay the whole immediately ;

(*u*) for treating any payment on account made by virtue of
paragraph (*t*) above as made on account of any benefit
to which this section applies that is subsequently
awarded or paid.

(2) This section applies to the following benefits—

(*a*) benefits under the Social Security Act 1975 ;   1975 c. 14.

(*b*) child benefit ;

(*c*) income support ;

(*d*) family credit ;

(*e*) housing benefit ;

(*f*) a payment under paragraph 2 of Schedule 6 to this Act (Christmas bonus) ;

and any social fund payments such as are mentioned in section 32(2)(*a*) above.

(3) Subsection (1)(*p*) above shall have effect in relation to housing benefit as if the reference to the Secretary of State were a reference to the authority paying the benefit.

(4) Subsection (1)(*g*), (*k*), (*n*), (*r*) and (*s*) above shall have effect as if statutory sick pay and statutory maternity pay were benefits to which this section applies.

Adjudication.

52.—(1) Part I of Schedule 5 to this Act (which makes amendments of enactments relating to social security adjudications) shall have effect.

1975 c. 14.

(2) The questions to which section 93(1) of the Social Security Act 1975 (questions for determination by the Secretary of State) applies shall include any question specified in Part II of that Schedule.

(3) Subject to subsections (7) and (8) below, the following provisions of the Social Security Act 1975 shall have effect for the purposes of the benefits to which this subsection applies as they have effect for the purposes of benefit under that Act—

    (*a*) sections 97 to 104 and 116 (adjudication officers, tribunals and Commissioners) ;

    (*b*) section 114 (regulations as to determination of questions) ;

    (*c*) section 115(1) and (2) and (4) to (7) and Schedule 13 (procedure) ;

    (*d*) section 117(1) and (2) (finality of decision) ;

    (*e*) section 119 (regulations in connection with adjudications) ; and

    (*f*) section 160 (age, marriage and death).

(4) Procedure regulations made under section 115 of the Social Security Act 1975 by virtue of subsection (3) above may make different provision in relation to each of the benefits to which subsection (3) above applies.

1982 c. 24.

(5) Section 148(1) of the Social Security Act 1975 (determinations of Secretary of State to be final) shall have effect in relation to offences under Part I of the Social Security and Housing Benefits Act 1982 and offences under this Act as it has effect in relation to offences under the Social Security Act 1975.

(6) Subsection (3) above applies to the following benefits—

    (*a*) child benefit ;

(*b*) statutory sick pay ;

(*c*) statutory maternity pay ;

(*d*) income support ;

(*e*) family credit ;

and any social fund payments such as are mentioned in section 32(2)(*a*) above.

(7) In their application to statutory sick pay and statutory maternity pay the provisions of the Social Security Act 1975 mentioned in subsection (3) above shall have effect as if— 1975 c. 14.

(*a*) the following subsection were substituted for section 98(1)—

" (1) Any question as to, or in connection with, entitlement to statutory sick pay or statutory maternity pay may be submitted to an adjudication officer—

(*a*) by the Secretary of State ; or

(*b*) subject to and in accordance with regulations, by the employee concerned,

for determination in accordance with sections 99 to 104 below." ;

(*b*) in section 99(3), for the words " notice in writing of the reference shall be given to the claimant " there were substituted the words " the employee and employer concerned shall each be given notice in writing of the reference." ;

(*c*) in section 100—

(i) in subsection (1), for the words " claimant may " there were substituted the words " employee and employer concerned shall each have a right to " ;

(ii) in subsection (2), for the words " claimant shall " there were substituted the words " employee and employer concerned shall each " ; and

(iii) subsection (7) were omitted ; and

(*d*) the following subsection were substituted for section 101(2) to (4)—

" (2) The persons at whose instance an appeal lies under this section are—

(*a*) an adjudication officer ;

(*b*) the employee concerned ;

(*c*) the employer concerned ;

(*d*) a trade union, or any other association which exists to promote the interests and welfare of its members, where—

C

(i) the employee is a member at the time of the appeal and was so immediately before the question at issue arose ; or

(ii) the question at issue is a question as to or in connection with entitlement of a deceased person who was at death a member ;

(e) an association of employers of which the employer is a member at the time of the appeal and was so immediately before the question at issue arose.".

1975 c. 14.

(8) In its application to family credit section 104(1)(*b*) of the Social Security Act 1975 shall have effect subject to section 20(6) above.

Over-payments.

53.—(1) Where it is determined that, whether fraudulently or otherwise, any person has misrepresented, or failed to disclose, any material fact and in consequence of the misrepresentation or failure—

(*a*) a payment has been made in respect of a benefit to which this section applies ; or

(*b*) any sum recoverable by or on behalf of the Secretary of State in connection with any such payment has not been recovered,

the Secretary of State shall be entitled to recover the amount of any payment which he would not have made or any sum which he would have received but for the misrepresentation or failure to disclose.

(2) An amount recoverable under subsection (1) above is in all cases recoverable from the person who misrepresented the fact or failed to disclose it.

(3) In relation to cases where payments of a benefit to which this section applies have been credited to a bank account or other account under arrangements made with the agreement of the beneficiary or a person acting for him, circumstances may be prescribed in which the Secretary of State is to be entitled to recover any amount paid in excess of entitlement ; but any such regulations shall not apply in relation to any payment unless before he agreed to the arrangements such notice of the effect of the regulations as may be prescribed was given in such manner as may be prescribed to the beneficiary or to a person acting for him.

(4) Except where regulations otherwise provide, an amount shall not be recoverable under subsection (1) above or regulations under subsection (3) above unless the determination in pursuance of which it was paid has been reversed or varied on an appeal or revised on a review.

(5) Regulations may provide—

   (*a*) that amounts recoverable under subsection (1) above or regulations under subsection (3) above shall be calculated or estimated in such manner and on such basis as may be prescribed :

   (*b*) for treating any amount paid to any person under an award which it is subsequently determined was not payable—

      (i) as properly paid ; or

      (ii) as paid on account of a payment which it is determined should be or should have been made,

   and for reducing or withholding any arrears payable by virtue of the subsequent determination ;

   (*c*) for treating any amount paid to one person in respect of another as properly paid for any period for which it is not payable in cases where in consequence of a subsequent determination—

      (i) the other person is himself entitled to a payment for that period ; or

      (ii) a third person is entitled in priority to the payee to a payment for that period in respect of the other person,

   and for reducing or withholding any arrears payable for that period by virtue of the subsequent determination.

(6) Circumstances may be prescribed in which a payment on account made by virtue of section 51(1)(*t*) above may be recovered to the extent that it exceeds entitlement.

(7) Where any amount paid is recoverable under—

   (*a*) section 27 above ;

   (*b*) subsection (1) above ; or

   (*c*) regulations under subsection (3) or (6) above,

it may, without prejudice to any other method of recovery, be recovered by deduction from prescribed benefits.

(8) Where any amount paid in respect of a married or unmarried couple is recoverable as mentioned in subsection (7) above, it may, without prejudice to any other method of recovery, be recovered, in such circumstances as may be prescribed, by deduction from prescribed benefits payable to either of them.

(9) Any amount recoverable under the provisions mentioned in subsection (7) above—

   (*a*) if the person from whom it is recoverable resides in England and Wales and the county court so orders, shall be recoverable by execution issued from the county court or otherwise as if it were payable under an order of that court ; and

    (*b*) if he resides in Scotland, shall be enforced in like manner as an extract registered decree arbitral bearing a warrant for execution issued by the sheriff court of any sheriffdom in Scotland.

(10) This section applies to the following benefits—

1975 c. 14.

    (*a*) benefits under the Social Security Act 1975 ;

    (*b*) child benefit ;

    (*c*) income support ;

    (*d*) family credit ;

and any social fund payments such as are mentioned in section 32(2)(*a*) above.

1975 c. 16.

(11) A scheme under section 2 or section 5 of the Industrial Injuries and Diseases (Old Cases) Act 1975 may make provision in relation to allowances under that Act corresponding to the provision made by this section in relation to the benefits to which it applies.

Breach of regulations.

54.—(1)Regulations under any of the benefit Acts may provide for contravention of, or failure to comply with, any provision contained in regulations made under that Act to be an offence under that Act and for the recovery, on summary conviction of any such offence, of penalties not exceeding—

    (*a*) for any one offence, level 3 on the standard scale ; or

    (*b*) for an offence of continuing any such contravention or failure after conviction, £40 for each day on which it is so continued.

(2) Subsection (1) above shall have effect in relation to the Industrial Injuries and Diseases (Old Cases) Act 1975 as if the references in that subsection to regulations were to schemes.

False representations for obtaining benefit etc.

55.—(1) If a person for the purpose of obtaining any benefit or other payment under any of the benefit Acts, whether for himself or some other person, or for any other purpose connected with any of those Acts—

    (*a*) makes a statement or representation which he knows to be false ; or

    (*b*) produces or furnishes, or knowingly causes or knowingly allows to be produced or furnished, any document or information which he knows to be false in a material particular,

he shall be guilty of an offence.

(2) A person guilty of an offence under subsection (1) above shall be liable on summary conviction to a fine not exceeding

level 5 on the standard scale, or to imprisonment for a term
not exceeding three months, or to both.

56.—(1) Any person authorised by the Secretary of State in Legal
that behalf may conduct any proceedings under the benefit Acts proceedings.
before a magistrates' court although not a barrister or solicitor.

(2) Notwithstanding·anything in any Act—

    (*a*) proceedings for an offence under the benefit Acts other
than an offence relating to housing benefit may be
begun at any time within the period of three months
from the date on which evidence, sufficient in the
opinion of the Secretary of State to justify a prosecution for the offence, comes to his knowledge or within
a period of twelve months from the commission of
the offence, whichever period last expires ; and

    (*b*) proceedings for an offence under the benefit Acts re-
lating to housing benefit may be begun at any time
within the period of three months from the date on
which evidence, sufficient in the opinion of the appropriate authority to justify a prosecution for the offence,
comes to the authority's knowledge or within a period
of twelve months from the commission of the offence,
whichever period last expires.

(3) For the purposes of subsection (2) above—

    (*a*) a certificate purporting to be signed by or on behalf
of the Secretary of State as to the date on which such
evidence as is mentioned in paragraph (*a*) of that subsection came to his knowledge shall be conclusive evidence of that date ; and

    (*b*) a certificate of the appropriate authority as to the date
on which such evidence as is mentioned in paragraph
(*b*) of that subsection came to the authority's knowledge shall be conclusive evidence of that date.

(4) In subsections (2) and (3) above " the appropriate authority " means, in relation to an offence concerning any dwelling—

    (*a*) if the offence relates to rate rebate, the authority who
are the appropriate rating authority by virtue of section 28(3) above ;

    (*b*) if it relates to a rent rebate, the authority who are the
appropriate housing authority by virtue of that subsection ; **and**

    (*c*) if it relates to rent allowance, the authority who are
the appropriate local authority by virtue of that subsection.

(5) In the application of this section to Scotland, the following provisions shall have effect in substitution for subsections (1) to (4) above—

    (*a*) proceedings for an offence under the benefit Acts may, notwithstanding anything in section 331 of the Criminal Procedure (Scotland) Act 1975, be commenced at any time within the period of three months from the date on which evidence sufficient in the opinion of the Lord Advocate to justify proceedings comes to his knowledge, or within the period of twelve months from the commission of the offence, whichever period last expires ;

    (*b*) for the purposes of this subsection—

        (i) a certificate purporting to be signed by or on behalf of the Lord Advocate as to the date on which such evidence as is mentioned above came to his knowledge shall be conclusive evidence thereof ;

        (ii) subsection (3) of section 331 of the said Act of 1975 (date of commencement of proceedings) shall have effect as it has effect for the purposes of that section.

Offences by bodies corporate.

57.—(1) Where an offence under any of the benefit Acts which has been committed by a body corporate is proved to have been committed with the consent or connivance of, or to be attributable to any neglect on the part of, a director, manager, secretary or other similar officer of the body corporate, or any person who was purporting to act in any such capacity, he, as well as the body corporate, shall be guilty of that offence and be liable to be proceeded against accordingly.

(2) Where the affairs of a body corporate are managed by its members, subsection (1) above applies in relation to the acts and defaults of a member in connection with his functions of management as if he were a director of the body corporate.

Inspection.

58.—(1) For the purposes of the benefit Acts, the Secretary of State may appoint such inspectors, and pay to them such salaries or remuneration, as he may determine with the consent of the Treasury.

(2) An inspector appointed under this section shall, for the purposes of the execution of the benefit Acts, have the following powers—

    (*a*) to enter at all reasonable times any premises liable to inspection under this section ;

    (*b*) to make such examination and enquiry as may be necessary—

        (i) for ascertaining whether the provisions of any of those Acts are being, or have been, complied with in any such premises ; or

(ii) for investigating the circumstances in which any injury or disease which has given or may give rise to a claim for industrial injuries benefit was or may have been received or contracted ;

(c) to examine, either alone or in the presence of any other person, as he thinks fit, in relation to any matters under any of those Acts on which he may reasonably require information, every person whom he finds in any such premises or whom he has reasonable cause to believe to be or to have been a person liable to pay—

(i) contributions under the Social Security Act 1975 ; 1975 c. 14.

(ii) a state scheme premium,

and to require every such person to be so examined ;

(d) to exercise such other powers as may be necessary for carrying any of the benefit Acts into effect.

(3) The premises liable to inspection under this section are any where an inspector has reasonable grounds for supposing that—

(a) any persons are employed ;

(b) there is being carried on any agency or other business for the introduction or supply to persons requiring them of persons available to do work or to perform services ; or

(c) a personal or occupational pension scheme is being administered,

but do not include any private dwelling-house not used by, or by permission of, the occupier for the purposes of a trade or business.

(4) Every inspector shall be furnished with a certificate of his appointment, and on applying for admission to any premises for the purpose of any of the benefit Acts shall, if so required, produce the certificate.

(5) Where any premises are liable to be inspected by an inspector or officer appointed or employed by, or are under the control of, some other government department, the Secretary of State may make arrangements with that department for any of the powers or duties of inspectors to be carried out by an inspector or officer employed by that department.

(6) In accordance with this section, persons shall furnish to an inspector all such information, and produce for his inspection

PART VI

1975 c. 14.

all such documents, as he may reasonably require for the purpose of ascertaining—

(a) whether—
(i) any contribution under the Social Security Act 1975 ;
(ii) any state scheme premium,
is or has been payable, or has been duly paid, by or in respect of any person ; or

(b) whether benefit under any of the benefit Acts is or was payable to or in respect of any person.

(7) The following persons are under the duty imposed by subsection (6) above—

(a) the occupier of any premises liable to inspection under this section ;

(b) any person who is or has been an employer or an employee within the meaning of any of the benefit Acts ;

(c) any person carrying on an agency or other business for the introduction or supply to persons requiring them of persons available to do work or perform services ;

(d) any person who is or has at any time been a trustee or manager of a personal or occupational pension scheme ;

(e) any person who is or has been liable to pay such contributions or premiums ;

(f) the servants or agents of any such person as is specified in any of the preceding paragraphs ;

but no-one shall be required under this section to answer any questions or to give any evidence tending to incriminate himself, or, in a case of a person who is married, his or her spouse.

(8) If a person—

(a) wilfully delays or obstructs an inspector in the exercise of any power under this Act ; or

(b) refuses or neglects to answer any question or to furnish any information or to produce any document when required to do so under this Act,

he shall be guilty of an offence and liable on summary conviction to a fine not exceeding level 3 on the standard scale.

(9) Where a person is convicted of an offence under subsection (8)(b) above and the refusal or neglect is continued by him after his conviction, he shall be guilty of a further offence and liable on summary conviction to a fine not exceeding £40 for each day on which it is so continued.

Disclosure of information.

59.—(1) No obligation as to secrecy imposed by statute or otherwise on a person employed in relation to the Inland Revenue shall prevent information obtained in connection with the assessment or collection of income tax from being disclosed to the Secretary of State, or the Department of Health and Social Services for Northern Ireland, or to an officer of either of them authorised to receive such information in connection with the operation of any of the benefit Acts or of any corresponding enactment of Northern Ireland legislation.

(2) In relation to persons who are carrying on or have carried on a trade, profession or vocation income from which is chargeable to tax under Case I or II of Schedule D, disclosure under subsection (1) above relating to that trade, profession or vocation shall be limited to information about the commencement or cessation of the trade, profession or vocation, but sufficient information may also be given to identify the persons concerned.

(3) Subsection (1) above extends only to disclosure by or under the authority of the Commissioners of Inland Revenue; and information which is the subject of disclosure to any person by virtue of that subsection shall not be further disclosed to any other person, except where the further disclosure is made—

    (a) to a person to whom disclosure could by virtue of this section have been made by or under the authority of the Commissioners of Inland Revenue;

    (b) for the purposes of any proceedings (civil or criminal) in connection with the operation of any of the benefit Acts or of any corresponding Northern Ireland legislation; or

    (c) for any purposes of Part III of the Social Security Act 1975 including that Part as extended by section 52(3) above, and any corresponding provisions of Northern Ireland legislation.

    1975 c. 14.

60.—(1) Regulations may provide that it shall be the duty of any of the following persons—   Regulations as to notification of deaths.

    (a) the Registrar General for England and Wales;

    (b) the Registrar General of Births, Deaths and Marriages for Scotland;

    (c) each registrar of births and deaths,

to furnish the Secretary of State, for the purpose of his functions under the benefit Acts and the functions of the Department of Health and Social Services in Northern Ireland under any corresponding Northern Ireland legislation, with the prescribed particulars of such deaths as may be prescribed.

(2) The regulations may make provision as to the manner in which and times at which the particulars are to be furnished.

Subordinate legislation

61.—(1) Nothing in any enactment shall require any proposals in respect of regulations to be referred to the Committee, the Council or the Board if—

> (a) it appears to the Secretary of State that by reason of the urgency of the matter it is inexpedient so to refer them ; or
>
> (b) the relevant advisory body have agreed that they shall not be referred.

(2) Where by virtue only of subsection (1)(a) above the Secretary of State makes regulations without proposals in respect of them having been referred, then, unless the relevant advisory body agree that this subsection shall not apply, he shall refer the regulations to that body as soon as practicable after making them.

(3) Where the Secretary of State—

> (a) has referred proposals to the Committee or the Board, he may make the proposed regulations before the Committee or Board have made their report ;
>
> (b) has referred proposals to the Council, he may make the proposed regulations before the Council have given their advice,

only if after the reference it appears to him that by reason of the urgency of the matter it is expedient to do so.

(4) Where by virtue of this section regulations are made before a report of the Committee or Board has been made, the Committee or Board shall consider them and make a report to the Secretary of State containing such recommendations with regard to the regulations as the Committee or Board think appropriate ; and a copy of any report made to the Secretary of State on the regulations shall be laid by him before each House of Parliament together, if the report contains recommendations, with a statement of the extent (if any) to which the Secretary of State proposes to give effect to the recommendations and, in so far as he does not propose to give effect to them, his reasons why not.

(5) Nothing in any enactment shall require the reference to the Committee, the Council or the Board of regulations made by virtue of an enactment contained in this Act or in an Act passed before this Act, if they are—

> (a) contained in a statutory instrument made before the end of a period of 12 months from the commencement of the enactment under which it is made ; or
>
> (b) contained in a statutory instrument which—
>
> > (i) states that it contains only provisions consequential on a specified enactment or such provisions and regulations made under that enactment ; and

(ii) is made before the end of a period of 12 months from the commencement of that enactment.

(6) Nothing in any enactment shall require the reference to the Committee, the Council or the Board of regulations made by virtue of an enactment contained in an Act passed after this Act, if they are—

(a) contained in a statutory instrument made before the end of the period of 6 months from the commencement of the enactment under which it is made ; or

(b) contained in a statutory instrument which—

(i) states that it contains only provisions consequential on a specified enactment or such provisions and regulations made under that enactment ; and

(ii) is made before the end of the period of 6 months from the commencement of that enactment,

unless the Act containing the enactment by virtue of which the regulations are made excludes this subsection in respect of the regulations.

(7) Subject to subsection (8) below, before making—

(a) regulations relating to housing benefit (other than regulations of which the effect is to increase any amount specified in regulations previously made) ;

(b) an order under section 28(10) or 30 above,

the Secretary of State shall consult with organisations appearing to him to be representative of the authorities concerned.

(8) Nothing in subsection (7) above shall require the Secretary of State to undertake consultations if—

(a) it appears to him that by reason of the urgency of the matter it is inexpedient to do so ; or

(b) the organisations have agreed that consultations should not be undertaken.

(9) Where the Secretary of State has undertaken such consultations, he may make any regulations or order to which the consultations relate without completing the consultations if it appears to him that by reason of the urgency of the matter it is expedient to do so.

(10) In this section—

" the Board " means the Occupational Pensions Board ;

" the Committee " means the Social Security Advisory Committee ;

" the Council " means the Industrial Injuries Advisory Council.

PART VI
Subordinate
legislation—
miscellaneous.
1975 c. 14.

62.—(1) The following subsection shall be inserted after sub-section (3) of section 166 of the Social Security Act 1975 (general provisions about orders and regulations)—

" (3A) Without prejudice to any specific provisions in this Act, a power conferred by this Act to make an Order in Council, regulations or an order includes power to provide for a person to exercise a discretion in dealing with any matter.".

1975 c. 61.

(2) The following subsection shall be inserted after subsection (7) of section 22 of the Child Benefit Act 1975 (regulations and orders)—

" (7A) Without prejudice to any specific provisions in this Act, a power conferred by this Act to make an Order in Council or regulations includes a power to provide for a person to exercise a discretion in dealing with any matter.".

(3) In subsection (1) of section 167 of the Social Security Act 1975 (Parliamentary control of orders and regulations)—

(a) for the words from the beginning to " namely " there shall be substituted the words " Subject to the provisions of this section, a statutory instrument containing (whether alone or with other provisions)—

(a) regulations made by virtue of " ;

(b) in paragraph (b), for the words " no order shall be made wholly or partly by virtue of " there shall be substituted the words " an order under " ;

(c) in paragraph (c), for the words " no order shall be made " there shall be substituted the words " an order " ; and

(d) for the words " unless a draft of the regulations or order " there shall be substituted the words " shall not be made unless a draft of the instrument ".

General provisions as to operation of social security

Annual
up-rating of
benefits.

63.—(1) The Secretary of State shall in each tax year review the sums—

(a) specified—

(i) in Schedule 4 to the Social Security Act 1975 ;

(ii) in section 30(1) of that Act ;

1975 c. 16.

(iii) in sections 2(6)(c) and 7(2)(b) of the Industrial Injuries and Diseases (Old Cases) Act 1975 ;

1975 c. 60.

(iv) in section 6(1)(a) of the Social Security Pensions Act 1975 ;

(b) which are the additional pensions in long-term benefits ;

(c) which are the increases in the rates of retirement pensions under Schedule 1 to the Social Security Pensions
Act 1975 ;

(d) which are—

(i) payable by virtue of section 35(6) of that Act
to a person who is also entitled to a Category A or
Category B retirement pension (including sums payable by virtue of section 36(3)) ; or

(ii) payable to such a person as part of his Category
A or Category B retirement pension by virtue of an
order made under this section by virtue of this paragraph or made under section 126A of the Social
Security Act 1975 ;

(e) specified in section 41(2B) of the Social Security Act
1975 ;

(f) specified by virtue of section 5(1) of the Child Benefit
Act 1975 ;

(g) specified in section 7(1) of the Social Security and Housing Benefits Act 1982 ;

(h) specified in regulations under section 48(3) above ;

(i) prescribed for the purposes of section 21(6)(a) above or
specified in regulations under section 22(1) above,

in order to determine whether they have retained their value in
relation to the general level of prices obtaining in Great Britain
estimated in such manner as the Secretary of State thinks fit.

(2) Where it appears to the Secretary of State that the general
level of prices is greater at the end of the period under review
than it was at the beginning of that period, he shall lay before
Parliament the draft of an up-rating order—

(a) which increases each of the sums to which subsection (3)
below applies by a percentage not less than the percentage by which the general level of prices is greater
at the end of the period than it was at the beginning ;
and

(b) if he considers it appropriate, having regard to the
national economic situation and any other matters
which he considers relevant, which also increases by
such percentage or percentages as he thinks fit any of
the sums mentioned in subsection (1) above but to which
subsection (3) below does not apply ; and

(c) stating the amount of any sums which are mentioned in
subsection (1) above but which the order does not
increase.

(3) This subsection applies to sums—

(a) specified in Part I, paragraph 1, 2, 3, 4 or 5 of Part III, Part IV or Part V of Schedule 4 to the Social Security Act 1975;

(b) mentioned in subsection (1)(a)(iii) or (iv), (b), (c) or (d) above.

(4) Subsection (2) above shall not require the Secretary of State to provide for an increase in any case in which it appears to him that the amount of the increase would be inconsiderable.

(5) The Secretary of State may, in providing for an increase in pursuance of subsection (2) above, adjust the amount of the increase so as to round any sum up or down to such extent as he thinks appropriate.

(6) Where subsection (2) above requires the Secretary of State to lay before Parliament the draft of an order increasing any sum that could be reduced under section 17(1) of the Child Benefit Act 1975, the order may make such alteration to that sum as reflects the combined effect of that increase and of any reduction that could be made under that subsection.

(7) An increase in a sum such as is specified in subsection (1)(d)(ii) above shall form part of the Category A or Category B retirement pension of the person to whom it is paid and an increase in a sum specified such as is specified in subsection (1)(d)(i) above shall be added to and form part of that pension but shall not form part of the sum increased.

(8) Where any increment under section 35(6) of the Social Security Pensions Act 1975—

(a) is increased in any tax year by an order under section 37A of that Act; and

(b) in that tax year also falls to be increased by an order under this section,

the increase under this section shall be the amount that would have been specified in the order, but for this subsection, less the amount of the increase under section 37A.

(9) Where sums are payable to a person by virtue of section 35(6) of the Social Security Pensions Act 1975 (including such sums payable by virtue of section 36(3) of that Act) during a period ending with the date on which he became entitled to a Category A or Category B retirement pension, then, for the purpose of determining the amount of his Category A or Category B retirement pension, orders made under this section during that period shall be deemed to have come into force (consecutively in the order in which they were made) on the date on which he became entitled to that pension.

(10) If the Secretary of State considers it appropriate to do so, he may include in the draft of an up-rating order, in addition to any other provisions, provisions increasing any of the sums for the time being specified in regulations under Part II of this Act.

(11) The Secretary of State shall lay with any draft order under this section a copy of a report by the Government Actuary giving the latter's opinion on the likely effect on the National Insurance Fund of such parts of the order as relate to sums payable out of that Fund.

(12) If a draft order laid before Parliament in pursuance of this section is approved by a resolution of each House, the Secretary of State shall make the order in the form of the draft.

(13) An order under this section—

    (a) shall be framed so as to bring the alterations to which it relates into force—

        (i) in the week beginning with the first Monday in the tax year ; or

        (ii) on such earlier date in April as may be specified in the order ;

    (b) shall make such transitional provision as the Secretary of State considers expedient in respect of periods of entitlement—

        (i) to statutory sick pay ;

        (ii) to family credit,

    running at the date when the alterations come into force.

64.—(1) This section applies where the rate of any relevant Effect of benefit is altered— alteration of rates of
    (a) by an Act subsequent to this Act ; benefit.

    (b) by an order under section 63 above ; or

    (c) in consequence of any such Act or order altering any maximum rate of benefit ;

and in this section " the commencing date " means the date fixed for payment of benefit at an altered rate to commence.

(2) Subject to such exceptions or conditions as may be prescribed where—

    (a) the weekly rate of a relevant benefit is altered to a fixed amount higher or lower than the previous amount ; and

    (b) before the commencing date an award of that benefit has been made (whether before or after the passing of the relevant Act or the making of the relevant order), except as respects any period falling before the commencing date, the benefit shall become payable at the altered rate without any claim being made for it in the case of an increase in the rate of benefit or any review of the award in the case of a decrease, and the award shall have effect accordingly.

(3) Where—

> (a) the weekly rate of a relevant benefit is altered ; and
>
> (b) before the commencing date (but after that date is fixed) an award is made of the benefit,

the award either may provide for the benefit to be paid as from the commencing date at the altered rate or may be expressed in terms of the rate appropriate at the date of the award.

(4) Where in consequence of the passing of an Act, or the making of an order, altering the rate of disablement pension under section 57 of the Social Security Act 1975, regulations are made varying the scale of disablement gratuities under subsection (5) of that section, the regulations may provide that the scale as varied shall apply only in cases where the period taken into account by the assessment of the extent of the disablement in respect of which the gratuity is awarded begins or began after such day as may be prescribed.

1975 c. 14.

(5) Subject to such exceptions or conditions as may be prescribed, where—

> (a) for any purpose of any Act or regulations the weekly rate at which a person contributes to the cost of providing for a child, or to the maintenance of an adult dependant, is to be calculated for a period beginning on or after the commencing date for an increase in the weekly rate of benefit ; but
>
> (b) account is to be taken of amounts referable to the period before the commencing date,

those amounts shall be treated as increased in proportion to the increase in the weekly rate of benefit.

(6) In this section " relevant benefit " means benefit under the Social Security Act 1975 or the Industrial Injuries and Diseases (Old Cases) Act 1975.

1975 c. 16.

Reciprocal arrangements.

65.—(1) At the end of subsection (4)(b) of section 142 of the Social Security Act 1975 (co-ordination with Northern Ireland) there shall be added " (but not so as to confer any double benefit) and for determining, in cases where rights accrue both in relation to Great Britain and in relation to Northern Ireland, which of those rights shall be available to the person concerned ".

(2) In subsection (1) of section 143 of that Act (reciprocity with other countries)—

(*a*) for the words from " reciprocity " to the end of paragraph (*c*) there shall be substituted the words " reciprocity in matters relating to payments for purposes
similar or comparable to the purposes of this Act " ;
and

(*b*) the words " relating to social security " shall be omitted.

(3) The words " relating to child benefit " shall be omitted
from subsection (1) of section 15 of the Child Benefit Act 1975
(reciprocal agreements with countries outside the United Kingdom). 1975 c. 61.

(4) Sections 14 and 15 of the Child Benefit Act 1975 (reciprocal arrangements with Northern Ireland and reciprocal
agreements with countries outside the United Kingdom) shall
have effect in relation to income support, family credit and
housing benefit as they have effect in relation to child benefit,
references in them to Part I of that Act being construed as including references to this Act.

PART VII

MISCELLANEOUS, GENERAL AND SUPPLEMENTARY

Miscellaneous

66. Schedule 6 to this Act (which makes provision relating
to payments for pensioners) shall have effect. Pensioners'
Christmas
bonus.

67.—(1) The following subsections shall be inserted after
subsection (1) of section 7 of the Social Security and Housing
Benefits Act 1982 (rate of payment of statutory sick pay)— Rates of
payments of
statutory sick
pay and
provisions as
to recovery.
1982 c. 24.

" (1A) The Secretary of State may by regulations—

(*a*) substitute alternative provisions for subsection (1)
(*a*) to (*c*) above ; and

(*b*) make such consequential amendments of any provision contained in this Act as appear to him to be
required.

(1B) A statutory instrument containing (whether alone or
with other provisions) regulations under subsection (1A)
above shall not be made unless a draft of the instrument has
been laid before Parliament and approved by a resolution of
each House.".

(2) The following paragraph shall be substituted for subsection (1A)(*a*) of section 9 of that Act (recovery by employers of
amounts paid by way of statutory sick pay)—

" (*a*) giving any employer who has made a payment of statutory sick pay a right, except in prescribed circumstances, to an amount, determined in such manner as may
be prescribed—

(i) by reference to secondary Class 1 contributions paid in respect of statutory sick pay ; or

(ii) by reference to the aggregate of secondary Class 1 contributions so paid and secondary Class 1 contributions paid in respect of statutory maternity pay ; ".

Liability of Secretary of State to pay statutory sick pay in prescribed circumstances.
1982 c. 24.

68. The following subsections shall be added at the end of section 1 of the Social Security and Housing Benefits Act 1982—

" (5) Circumstances may be prescribed in which, notwithstanding the foregoing provisions of this section, the liability to make payments of statutory sick pay is to be a liability of the Secretary of State.

(6) Any sums paid under regulations made by virtue of subsection (5) above shall be paid out of the National Insurance Fund.".

Repeal of section 92 of Social Security Act 1975.
1975 c. 14.

69. Section 92 of the Social Security Act 1975 (which relates to arrangements to forgo benefit in return for unabated sick pay) shall cease to have effect.

Child benefit in respect of children educated otherwise than at educational establishments.
1975 c. 61.

70.—(1) In section 2 of the Child Benefit Act 1975 (meaning of " child ")—

(a) in paragraph (b) of subsection (1), for the words " by attendance at a recognised educational establishment " there shall be substituted the words " either by attendance at a recognised educational establishment or, if the education is recognised by the Secretary of State, elsewhere " ; and

(b) the following subsections shall be inserted after that subsection—

" (1A) The Secretary of State may recognise education provided otherwise than at a recognised educational establishment for a person who, in the opinion of the Secretary of State, could reasonably be expected to attend such an establishment only if the Secretary of State is satisfied that education was being so provided for that person immediately before he attained the age of sixteen.

(1B) Regulations may prescribe the circumstances in which education is or is not to be treated for the purposes of this Act as full-time.".

(2) Regulations purporting to be made under section 24(1) of that Act and made before the passing of this Act shall be treated as validly made.

71.—(1) In paragraph (*a*) of section 37A(2) of the Social Security Act 1975 (duration of inability or virtual inability to walk for the purposes of entitlement to mobility allowance) for the words " time when a claim for the allowance is received by the Secretary of State " there shall be substituted the words " relevant date ".

PART VII
Entitlement to mobility allowance—general.
1975 c. 14.

(2) The following subsections shall be inserted after that subsection—

"(2A) Subject to subsection (2B) below, in subsection (2)(*a*) above " the relevant date " means the date on which the claimant's inability or virtual inability to walk commenced or the date on which his claim was received or treated as received by the Secretary of State, whichever is the later.

(2B) Where—

(*a*) a claimant is awarded an allowance for a period ; and

(*b*) he subsequently claims an allowance for a further period,

the relevant date is the first date not earlier than the end of the period for which the allowance was awarded on which the claimant was unable or virtually unable to walk.

(2C) Regulations may make provision—

(*a*) for permitting an award on a claim for a mobility allowance to be made either as from the date on which the claim is received or treated as received by the Secretary of State or for a period beginning after that date subject to the condition that the person in respect of whom the claim is made satisfies the prescribed requirements for entitlement when benefit becomes payable under the award ;

(*b*) for the review of any such award if those requirements are found not to have been satisfied.".

(3) Section 37A(7) (under which, except so far as may be provided by regulations, the question of a person's entitlement to a mobility allowance falls to be determined as at the time when a claim for the allowance is received by the Secretary of State) shall cease to have effect.

(4) Where—

(*a*) it has been determined that a person was entitled to mobility allowance ; and

(*b*) the claim should have been determined as at the date

when it was received by the Secretary of State, but was determined as at a later date,

the fact that the claim was determined as at that date shall not invalidate the determination.

(5) Where the Secretary of State has made a payment to a person who has claimed mobility allowance on the ground that, if the person's claim had been received by the Secretary of State at a date later than that on which it was in fact received, the person would have been entitled to mobility allowance—

(*a*) the payment shall be treated as a payment of mobility allowance ; and

(*b*) the person shall be treated as having been entitled to mobility allowance for the period in respect of which the payment was made.

Entitlement of certain women to mobility allowance.
1975 c. 60.
1979 c. 18.

72. In relation to women born after 6th June 1918 but before 21st December 1919 sections 22 and 65(1) of the Social Security Pensions Act 1975, paragraphs 47, 49 and 51 to 53 of Schedule 4 to that Act and section 3(3) of the Social Security Act 1979 shall be deemed to have come into force—

(*a*) for the purposes of the making of claims for, and the determination of claims and questions relating to, mobility allowance, on 29th March 1979 ; and

(*b*) for all other purposes, on 6th June 1979.

Application of provisions of Act to supplementary benefit etc.

73. Schedule 7 to this Act shall have effect for the purpose of making provision in relation to the benefits there mentioned.

National Insurance contributions.
1975 c. 14.

74.—(1) The subsection set out in subsection (2) below shall be inserted in the Social Security Act 1975—

(*a*) in section 4 (Class 1 contributions) after subsection (6H), as subsection (6HH) ; and

(*b*) in section 123A (further power to alter certain contributions) after subsection (6), as subsection (6A).

(2) The subsection is—

" Where the Secretary of State lays before Parliament a draft of an order under this section he shall lay with it a copy of a report by the Government Actuary on the effect which, in the Actuary's opinion, the making of such an order may be expected to have on the National Insurance Fund.".

(3) In section 134 of that Act (appropriate employment protection allocation) the following subsections shall be inserted after subsection (5)—

" (5A) Without prejudice to section 122(3) and (4) above, the Secretary of State may, with the consent of the Treasury, by order amend this section, in relation to any tax year beginning after the tax year 1986-87—

(a) by substituting a different percentage for the percentage for the time being specified in paragraph (i) or (ii) of subsection (4) above or for each of the percentages specified in those paragraphs;

(b) by directing that there shall be no appropriate employment protection allocation; or

(c) by directing that there shall be an appropriate employment protection allocation only in the case of primary Class 1 contributions or only in the case of secondary Class 1 contributions.

(5B) At any time when an order under subsection (5A) above containing a direction under paragraph (b) of that subsection is in force, the Secretary of State may, with the consent of the Treasury, by order direct that there shall be an appropriate employment protection allocation of such percentage in the case of primary Class 1 contributions or secondary Class 1 contributions, or both, as may be specified in the order.

(5C) At any time when an order under subsection (5A) above containing a direction under paragraph (c) of that subsection is in force, the Secretary of State may, with the consent of the Treasury, by order direct that there shall be an appropriate employment protection allocation of such percentage as may be specified in the order in the case of the description of contributions in whose case there is, by virtue of the direction, no such allocation.

(5D) Any percentage specified as an allocation by an order under subsection (5B) or (5C) above shall be deemed to be inserted at the appropriate place in subsection (4) above and an order under subsection (5A)(a) above may accordingly be made in respect of it.".

(4) In section 167(1)(b) of that Act (orders subject to affirmative procedure) after " 134 (4A) " there shall be inserted " (5A), (5B) or (5C) ".

(5) The powers to prescribe equivalents of a limit or bracket under section 4 of and paragraph 1(1C) of Schedule 1 to that Act include power to prescribe an amount not more than £1·00 more than the amount which is the arithmetical equivalent of the limit or bracket.

(6) In section 1(2) of the Social Security Pensions Act 1975 (lower earnings limit) for " 49p " there shall be substituted " 99p ".

1975 c. 60.

PART VII
Earnings
factors.

1977 c. 5.

75. The Social Security Acts 1975 and the Social Security (Miscellaneous Provisions) Act 1977 shall be amended in accordance with Schedule 8 to this Act in relation to earnings factors for the tax year in which this section comes into force and subsequent tax years.

Amendments
relating to
forfeiture of
benefits.

1982 c. 34.

76.—(1) The Forfeiture Act 1982 shall be amended as follows.

(2) The following subsections shall be inserted after subsection (1) of section 4 (Social Security Commissioner to determine whether forfeiture rule applies to social security benefits)—

" (1A) Where a Commissioner determines that the forfeiture rule has precluded a person (in this section referred to as " the offender ") who has unlawfully killed another from receiving the whole or part of any such benefit or advantage, the Commissioner may make a decision under this subsection modifying the effect of that rule and may do so whether the unlawful killing occurred before or after the coming into force of this subsection.

(1B) The Commissioner shall not make a decision under subsection (1A) above modifying the effect of the forfeiture rule in any case unless he is satisfied that, having regard to the conduct of the offender and of the deceased and to such other circumstances as appear to the Commissioner to be material, the justice of the case requires the effect of the rule to be so modified in that case.

(1C) Subject to subsection (1D) below, a decision under subsection (1A) above may modify the effect of the forfeiture rule in either or both of the following ways—

(*a*) so that it applies only in respect of a specified proportion of the benefit or advantage ;

(*b*) so that it applies in respect of the benefit or advantage only for a specified period of time.

(1D) Such a decision may not modify the effect of the forfeiture rule so as to allow any person to receive the whole or any part of a benefit or advantage in respect of any period before the commencement of this subsection.

(1E) If the Commissioner thinks it expedient to do so, he may direct that his decision shall apply to any future claim for a benefit or advantage under a relevant enactment, on which a question such as is mentioned in subsection (1) above arises by reason of the same unlawful killing.

(1F) It is immaterial for the purposes of subsection (1E) above whether the claim is in respect of the same or a different benefit or advantage.

(1G) For the purpose of obtaining a decision whether the forfeiture rule should be modified the Secretary of State may refer to a Commissioner for review any determination of a question such as is mentioned in subsection (1) above that was made before the commencement of subsections (1A) to (1F) above (whether by a Commissioner or not) and shall do so if the offender requests him to refer such a determination.

(1H) Subsections (1A) to (1F) above shall have effect on a reference under subsection (1G) above as if in subsection (1A) the words " it has been determined " were substituted for the words " a Commissioner determines ".".

(3) In subsection (2) of that section, after the words " that subsection " there shall be inserted the words " or any decision under subsection (1A) above ".

(4) In section 5 (exclusion of murderers) after the word " Act ", in the second place where it occurs, there shall be inserted the words " or in any decision made under section 4(1A) of this Act ".

77.—(1) The words " and may do so either on the premises or Refreshments at any place other than the school premises where education is for school being provided " shall be inserted— pupils.

> (*a*) after " refreshment " in subsection (1)(*a*) of section 22
>   of the Education Act 1980 ; and   1980 c. 20.
> (*b*) after " management " in subsection (1)(*a*) of section 53
>   of the Education (Scotland) Act 1980.   1980 c. 44.

(2) The following subsections shall be substituted for subsections (2) and (3) of each of those sections—

" (2) Subject to subsection (3) below, an authority must charge for anything provided by them under subsection (1)(*a*) above and must charge every pupil the same price for the same quantity of the same item.

(3) In relation to a pupil whose parents are in receipt of income support or who is himself in receipt of it an authority shall so exercise the power conferred by subsection (1)(*a*) above as to ensure that such provision is made for him in the middle of the day as appears to the authority to be requisite and shall make that provision for him free of charge.".

78. The Secretary of State may pay such travelling expenses Travelling as, with the consent of the Treasury, he may determine— expenses.

> (*a*) to persons required by him to attend an interview in
>   connection with the operation of any of the benefit
>   Acts ;

(*b*) to persons attending local offices in connection with the operation—

        (i) of any of those Acts ; or

        (ii) of any prescribed enactment.

General

Crown
employment.

79.—(1) A person who is employed by or under the Crown shall be treated as an employed earner for the purposes of sections 1 to 17 above.

(2) A person who is serving as a member of Her Majesty's forces shall, while he is so serving, be treated for the purposes of sections 1 to 16 above as an employed earner in respect of his membership of those forces.

(3) The provisions of this Act relating to family credit apply in relation to persons employed by or under the Crown as they apply in relation to persons employed otherwise than by or under the Crown.

(4) Subject to subsection (5) below, the provisions of Part V of this Act apply in relation to persons employed by or under the Crown as they apply in relation to persons employed otherwise than by or under the Crown.

(5) The provisions of that Part of this Act do not apply in relation to persons serving as members of Her Majesty's forces, in their capacity as such.

(6) For the purposes of this section Her Majesty's forces shall be taken to consist of such establishments and organisations as may be prescribed, being establishments and organisations in which persons serve under the control of the Defence Council.

Application
of Parts I and
V to special
cases.

80.—(1) Regulations may modify Parts I and V of this Act, in such manner as the Secretary of State thinks proper, in their application to any person who is, or has been, or is to be—

    (*a*) employed on board any ship, vessel, hovercraft or aircraft ;

    (*b*) outside Great Britain at any prescribed time or in any prescribed circumstances ; or

    (*c*) in prescribed employment in connection with continental shelf operations.

(2) Regulations under subsection (1) above may in particular provide—

    (*a*) for any provision of either of those Parts of this Act to apply to any such person, notwithstanding that it would not otherwise apply ;

    (*b*) for any such provision not to apply to any such person, notwithstanding that it would otherwise apply ;

(c) for excepting any such person from the application of any such provision where he neither is domiciled nor has a place of residence in any part of Great Britain :

(d) for the taking of evidence, for the purposes of the determination of any question arising under any such provision, in a country or territory outside Great Britain, by a British consular official or such other person as may be determined.

(3) In this section " continental shelf operations " means any activities which, if paragraphs (a) and (d) of subsection (6) of section 23 of the Oil and Gas (Enterprise) Act 1982 (application of civil law to certain off-shore activities) were omitted, would nevertheless fall within subsection (2) of that section.

PART VII

1982 c. 23.

Northern Ireland

81. An Order in Council under paragraph 1(1)(b) of Schedule 1 to the Northern Ireland Act 1974 (legislation for Northern Ireland in the interim period) which states that it is made only for purposes corresponding to those of this Act—

(a) shall not be subject to paragraph 1(4) and (5) of that Schedule (affirmative resolution of both Houses of Parliament) ; but

(b) shall be subject to annulment in pursuance of a resolution of either House.

Orders in Council making corresponding provision for Northern Ireland.
1974 c. 28.

82. The enactments relating to social security in Northern Ireland specified in Schedule 9 to this Act shall have effect subject to the amendments there specified.

Amendments of enactments relating to social security in Northern Ireland.

Supplementary

83.—(1) Section 166(1) to (3A) of the Social Security Act 1975 (extent of powers) shall apply to powers conferred by this Act to make regulations or orders as they apply to any power to make regulations or orders conferred by that Act but as if for references to that Act there were substituted references to this Act.

Orders and regulations (general provisions).
1975 c. 14.

(2) Any power conferred by this Act to make orders or regulations relating to housing benefit shall include power to make different provision for different areas.

(3) A statutory instrument containing (whether alone or with other provisions)—

(a) regulations under section 5(15)(a) above ;

(b) regulations under Part II of this Act which are made before the coming into operation of that Part ;

(c) orders under section 30(2) or (3) above which are made before the coming into operation of those subsections ;

(*d*) an order under section 63 above ;

(*e*) an order under paragraph 2(3)(*b*) of Schedule 6 to this Act,

shall not be made unless a draft of the instrument has been laid before Parliament and approved by a resolution of each House.

(4) All regulations and orders made under this Act, other than those to which subsection (3) above applies and orders under section 88 below, shall be subject to annulment in pursuance of a resolution of either House of Parliament.

(5) An order under section 30 or 63 above or section 85 below shall not be made without the consent of the Treasury.

(6) A power conferred by this Act to make any regulations or order, where the power is not expressed to be exercisable with the consent of the Treasury, shall if the Treasury so direct be exercisable only in conjunction with them.

General interpretation.

84.—(1) In this Act, unless the context othewise requires,—

" applicable amount " shall be construed in accordance with Part II of this Act ;

" average salary benefits " means benefits the rate or amount of which is calculated by reference to the average salary of a member of a pension scheme over the period of service on which the benefits are based ;

" the benefit Acts " means—

1973 c. 38.   (*a*) the Social Security Act 1973 ;

(*b*) the Social Security Acts 1975 to 1986 ;

1975 c. 16.   (*c*) the Industrial Injuries and Diseases (Old Cases) Act 1975 ;

1975 c. 61.   (*d*) the Child Benefit Act 1975 ;

1975 c. 14.   " contract of service " has the same meaning as in the Social Security Act 1975 ;

" dwelling " means any residential accommodation, whether or not consisting of the whole or part of a building and whether or not comprising separate and self-contained premises ;

" employed earner " has the same meaning as in the Social Security Act 1975 ;

" employee " means a person gainfully employed in Great Britain either under a contract of service or in an office (including an elective office) with emoluments chargeable to income tax under Schedule E ;

" employer " means—

(*a*) in the case of an employed earner employed under a contract of service, his employer ;

(*b*) in the case of an employed earner employed in an office with emoluments—

(i) such person as may be prescribed in relation to that office ; or

(ii) if no person is prescribed, the government department, public authority or body of persons responsible for paying the emoluments of the office ;

" housing authority " means a local authority, a new town corporation, the Scottish Special Housing Association or the Development Board for Rural Wales ;

" housing benefit scheme " shall be construed in accordance with Part II of this Act ;

" Housing Revenue Account dwelling ", in relation to a local authority, means a dwelling which is within the authority's Housing Revenue Account (within the meaning of Part XIII of the Housing Act 1985) and is not— 1985 c. 68.

(*a*) a dwelling for the time being let on a long tenancy at a low rent within the meaning of the Leasehold Reform Act 1967 ; or 1967 c. 88.

(*b*) a dwelling no longer owned by the authority ;

" Housing Revenue Account rebate ", in relation to a local authority in England and Wales, means a rent rebate for a tenant of a Housing Revenue Account dwelling of that authority ;

" income-related benefit " shall be construed in accordance with Part II of this Act ;

" insurance company " has the meaning assigned to it by section 96(1) of the Insurance Companies Act 1982 ; 1982 c. 50.

" local authority " means—

(*a*) in relation to England and Wales, the council of a district or London borough, the Common Council of the City of London or the Council of the Isles of Scilly ; and

(*b*) in relation to Scotland, an islands or district council ;

" long-term benefit " has the meaning assigned to it by Schedule 20 to the Social Security Act 1975 ; 1975 c. 14.

" minimum contributions " shall be construed in accordance with Part I of this Act ;

" modifications " includes additions, omissions and amendments, and related expressions shall be construed accordingly ;

" money purchase benefits ", in relation to a member of a personal or occupational pension scheme or the widow or widower of a member of such a scheme, means benefits the rate or amount of which is calculated by reference to a payment or payments made by the member or by any other person in respect of the member and which are not average salary benefits ;

" new town corporation " means—

1981 c. 64.
(a) in relation to England and Wales, a development corporation established under the New Towns Act 1981 or the Commission for the New Towns ; and

1968 c. 16.
(b) in relation to Scotland, a development corporation established under the New Towns (Scotland) Act 1968 ;

1975 c. 60.
" occupational pension scheme " has the same meaning as in section 66(1) of the Social Security Pensions Act 1975 ;

" personal pension scheme " means any scheme or arrangement which is comprised in one or more instruments or agreements and which has, or is capable of having, effect so as to provide benefits, in the form of pensions or otherwise, payable on death or retirement to or in respect of employed earners who have made arrangements with the trustees or managers of the scheme for them to become members of the scheme ;

" prescribed " means specified in or determined in accordance with regulations ;

" primary Class 1 contributions " and " secondary Class 1 contributions " have the same meanings as in the
1975 c. 14.
Social Security Act 1975 ;

" protected rights " shall be construed in accordance with Schedule 1 to this Act ;

" qualifying benefit " has the meaning assigned to it by Schedule 6 to this Act ;

" rate rebate ", " rent rebate " and " rent allowance " shall be construed in accordance with section 28 above ;

" rates " and " rating authority "—

1967 c. 9.
(a) in relation to England and Wales, have the same meaning as in the General Rate Act 1967 ; and

(b) in relation to Scotland, have respectively the same meanings as " rate " has in section 379 of the
1947 c. 43.
Local Government (Scotland) Act 1947 and " rat-
1973 c. 65.
ing authority " has in section 109 of the Local Government (Scotland) Act 1973 ;

" regulations " means regulations made by the Secretary of State under this Act ;

" social fund payment " means a payment under Part III of this Act ;

" tax-exemption " and " tax-approval " mean respectively exemption from tax and approval of the Inland Revenue in either case under any such provision of the Income Tax Acts as may be prescribed ;

" tax year " means the 12 months beginning with 6th April in any year ;

" trade dispute " has the same meaning as in the Social Security Act 1975 ; 1975 c. 14.

" war disablement pension " means—

(*a*) any retired pay, pension or allowance granted in respect of disablement under powers conferred by or under the Air Force (Constitution) Act 1917, the Personal Injuries (Emergency Provisions) Act 1939, the Pensions (Navy, Army, Air Force and Mercantile Marine) Act 1939, the Polish Resettlement Act 1947, or Part VII or section 151 of the Reserve Forces Act 1980 ; 1917 c. 51. 1939 c. 82. 1939 c. 83. 1947 c. 19. 1980 c. 9.

(*b*) without prejudice to paragraph (*a*) of this definition, any retired pay or pension to which subsection (1) of section 365 of the Income and Corporation Taxes Act 1970 applies ; 1970 c. 10.

" war widow's pension " means any widow's pension or allowance granted in respect of a death due to service or war injury and payable by virtue of any enactment mentioned in paragraph (*a*) of the preceding definition or a pension or allowance for a widow granted under any scheme mentioned in subsection (2)(*e*) of the said section 365.

(2) Expressions used in Part I of this Act and in the Social Security Pensions Act 1975 have the same meanings in that Part as they have in that Act. 1975 c. 60.

(3) References in this Act to the general rate fund of an authority shall be construed—

(*a*) in relation to the Council of the Isles of Scilly, as references to their general fund ; and

(*b*) in relation to the Common Council of the City of London, as references to their general rate.

(4) In this Act—

(*a*) references to the United Kingdom include references to the territorial waters of the United Kingdom ; and

(*b*) references to Great Britain include references to the territorial waters of the United Kingdom adjacent to Great Britain.

85.—(1) There shall be paid out of money provided by Parliament—

> (*a*) any sums payable by way of the following—
>> (i) income support ;
>> (ii) family credit ;
>> (iii) rate rebate subsidy ;
>> (iv) rent rebate subsidy ;
>> (v) rent allowance subsidy ;
>
> (*b*) payments by the Secretary of State into the social fund ;
>
> (*c*) any sum payable to a person under Schedule 6 to this Act if the relevant qualifying benefit to which he is entitled or treated as entitled is a benefit payable out of such money ;
>
> (*d*) any sums falling to be paid by the Secretary of State under or by virtue of this Act by way of travelling expenses ;
>
> (*e*) any other expenses of the Secretary of State attributable to this Act ;
>
> (*f*) any expenses of the Lord Chancellor attributable to this Act ; and
>
> (*g*) any increase attributable to this Act in the sums payable out of money provided by Parliament under any other Act.

(2) Any increase attributable to this Act in the sums to be charged on and paid out of the Consolidated Fund under any other Act shall be charged on and paid out of that Fund.

(3) There shall be paid out of the National Insurance Fund—

> (*a*) minimum contributions paid by the Secretary of State under Part I of this Act ;
>
> (*b*) payments by him under section 7 above ;
>
> (*c*) sums falling to be paid by or on behalf of the Secretary of State under regulations made by virtue of section 46(8)(*b*) above or paragraph 1(*b*) or (*e*) of Schedule 4 to this Act ; and
>
> (*d*) any sums paid to a person under Schedule 6 to this Act if the relevant qualifying benefit to which the person is entitled or treated as entitled is a benefit payable out of that fund.

(4) There shall be paid out of the National Insurance Fund into the Consolidated Fund, at such times and in such manner as the Treasury may direct, such sums as the Secretary of State may estimate (in accordance with any directions given by the Treasury)—

> (*a*) to be the amount of the administrative expenses incurred by the Secretary of State under Part V of this Act,

excluding any category of expenses which the Treasury may direct, or any enactment may require, to be excluded from the Secretary of State's estimate under this subsection ; and

(b) to be the amount of the administrative expenses incurred by a government department under Schedule 6 to this Act.

(5) Subject to subsections (6) and (7) below, so far as it relates to payments out of money provided by Parliament, any sum recovered by the Secretary of State under or by virtue of this Act shall be paid into the Consolidated Fund.

(6) So far as any such sum relates to a payment out of the National Insurance Fund, it shall be paid into that Fund.

(7) So far as any such sum relates to a payment out of the social fund, it shall be paid into that fund.

(8) There shall also be paid into the National Insurance Fund sums recovered under section 1(6) or (7) or 7(8) or (9) above any personal pension protected rights premium and sums recovered by the Secretary of State by virtue of a scheme under section 2 or section 5 of the Industrial Injuries and Diseases (Old 1975 c. 16. Cases) Act 1975 making provision corresponding to that made by or by virtue of this Act.

(9) There shall be made out of the National Insurance Fund into the Consolidated Fund or out of money provided by Parliament into the National Insurance Fund such payments by way of adjustment as the Secretary of State determines (in accordance with any direction of the Treasury) to be appropriate in consequence of the operation of any enactment or regulations relating to family credit, statutory sick pay or statutory maternity pay.

(10) Where such adjustments fall to be made, the amount of the payments to be made shall be taken to be such, in such cases or classes of case as may be specified by the Secretary of State by order, and payments on account thereof shall be made at such times and in such manner, as may be determined by the Secretary of State in accordance with any direction given by the Treasury.

(11) There shall be made—

(a) out of the social fund into the Consolidated Fund or the National Insurance Fund ;

(b) into the social fund out of money provided by Parliament or the National Insurance Fund,

such payments by way of adjustment as the Secretary of State determines (in accordance with any directions of the Treasury) to be appropriate in consequence of any enactment or regulations relating to the repayment or offsetting of a benefit under any of the benefit Acts or other payments under any of those Acts.

(12) Where in any other circumstances payments fall to be made by way of adjustment—

    (*a*) out of the social fund into the Consolidated Fund or the National Insurance Fund ; or

    (*b*) into the social fund out of money provided by Parliament or the National Insurance Fund,

then, in such cases or classes of case as may be specified by the Secretary of State by order, the amount of the payments to be made shall be taken to be such, and payments on account of it shall be made at such times and in such manner, as may be determined by the Secretary of State in accordance with any direction given by the Treasury.

(13) In this section " Act " includes an Act of the Parliament of Northern Ireland.

Minor and consequential amendments and repeals.

86.—(1) The enactments mentioned in Schedule 10 to this Act shall have effect with the amendments there specified.

(2) The enactments mentioned in Schedule 11 to this Act (which include enactments already obsolete or unnecessary) are repealed to the extent specified in the third column of that Schedule.

Extent.

87.—(1) The following provisions of this Act extend to Northern Ireland—

    (*a*) section 17(2) above, so far as relating to Acts which extend to Northern Ireland ;

    (*b*) section 61 above ;

    (*c*) section 66 above, so far as relating to paragraph 3(6) of Schedule 6 ;

    (*d*) section 81 above ;

    (*e*) sections 83 to 86 above ;

    (*f*) this section ;

    (*g*) sections 88 to 90 below.

(2) Section 82 above (with Schedule 9) extends to Northern Ireland only.

(3) Sections 25 and 30(6) and (10) above do not extend to Scotland.

(4) Where any enactment repealed or amended by this Act extends to any part of the United Kingdom, the repeal or amendment extends to that part.

(5) Except as provided by this section, this Act extends to England and Wales and Scotland, but not to Northern Ireland.

88.—(1) Subject to the following provisions of this section, the Commence-provisions of this Act shall come into force on such day as the ment. Secretary of State may by order made by statutory instrument appoint, and different days may be appointed in pursuance of this section for different provisions or different purposes of the same provision.

(2) In relation to section 52 above (including Schedule 5) and section 82 above (including Schedule 9) for the reference to the Secretary of State in subsection (1) above there shall be substituted a reference to the Lord Chancellor and the Secretary of State, acting jointly.

(3) Without prejudice to the generality of subsection (1) above, different days may be appointed under that subsection for the purposes of Part III of this Act in relation to different descriptions of persons, and those descriptions of persons may be determined by any criteria that appear to the Secretary of State to be appropriate.

(4) If an order under subsection (1) above brings paragraph 8 of Schedule 3 to this Act into force on the same day as section 36 above, the former shall be deemed to have come into force immediately before the latter.

(5) The following provisions of this Act—

section 30(4), (8), (9) and (10) ;
section 37 ;
section 38(4) ;
section 45 ;
section 61 ;
sections 63 and 64 ;
section 70 ;
section 71(4) and (5) ;
section 72 ;
section 74 ;
section 76 ;
section 81 ;
section 83 to 85 ;
section 86(1) so far as relating to paragraphs 2, 22, 23(3), 26(1) and (2), 27, 30(*b*), (*c*) and (*d*)(ii), 82, 86, 94(*a*), 98, 99, 106 and 107 of Schedule 10 ;

PART VII
1975 c. 14.

1977 c. 5.

1975 c. 60.

1980 c. 30.

1982 c. 24.

section 86(2) so far as relating—

   (*a*) to section 37(3) of the Social Security Act 1975 and the reference to paragraph (*b*) of that subsection in section 22(2) of the Social Security (Miscellaneous Provisions) Act 1977 ;

   (*b*) to section 141(2) of the Social Security Act 1975 ;

   (*c*) to section 52D(2) and (3) of the Social Security Pensions Act 1975 and paragraph 12 of Schedule 1A to that Act ;

   (*d*) to section 10 of the Social Security Act 1980 ; and

   (*e*) to section 29 of the Social Security and Housing Benefits Act 1982 ;

section 87 ;

this section ; and

sections 89 and 90 :

shall come into force on the day this Act is passed.

Transitional.   **89.**—(1) Regulations may make such transitional and consequential provision (including provision modifying any enactment contained in this or any other Act) or saving as the Secretary of State considers necessary or expedient in preparation for or in connection with the coming into force of any provision of this Act or the operation of any enactment which is repealed or amended by a provision of this Act during any period when the repeal or amendment is not wholly in force.

(2) The reference to regulations in subsection (1) above includes a reference—

   (*a*) to regulations made by the Lord Chancellor ; and

   (*b*) to regulations made by the Lord Chancellor and the Secretary of State, acting jointly.

Citation.   **90.**—(1) This Act may be cited as the Social Security Act 1986.

(2) This Act, except section 77 above, may be cited together with the Social Security Acts 1975 to 1985 as the Social Security Acts 1975 to 1986.

SCHEDULES

SCHEDULE 1

APPROPRIATE PERSONAL PENSION SCHEMES

Interpretation

1. In this Schedule—

" member " means a member of a scheme ;

" rules " means the rules of a scheme ; and

" scheme " means a personal pension scheme.

Requirements : general

2. The Secretary of State may prescribe descriptions of persons by whom or bodies by which a scheme may be established and, if he does so, a scheme may only be established by a person or body of a prescribed description.

3. A scheme must comply with such requirements as may be prescribed as regards the investment of its resources and with any direction of the Occupational Pensions Board that—

(*a*) no part, or no more than a specified proportion, of the scheme's resources shall be invested in investments of a specified class or description ;

(*b*) there shall be realised, before the end of a specified period, the whole or a specified proportion of investments of a specified class or description forming part of the scheme's resources when the direction is given.

4. A scheme must comply with such requirements as may be prescribed as regards the part—

(*a*) of any payment or payments that are made to the scheme by or on behalf of a member ;

(*b*) of any income or capital gain arising from the investment of payments such as are mentioned in sub-paragraph (*a*) above ; or

(*c*) of the value of rights under the scheme,

that may be used—

(i) to defray the administrative expenses of the scheme ;

(ii) to pay commission ; or

(iii) in any other way which does not result in the provision of benefits for or in respect of members.

5.—(1) Subject to sub-paragraph (2) below, all minimum contributions which are paid to a scheme in respect of one of its members must be applied so as to provide money purchase benefits for or in respect of that member, except so far as they are used—

(*a*) to defray the administrative expenses of the scheme ; or

(*b*) to pay commission.

(2) If regulations are made under paragraph 4 above, minimum contributions may be used in any way which the regulations permit, but not in any way not so permitted except to provide money purchase benefits for or in respect of the member.

6. A scheme must satisfy such other requirements as may be prescribed.

Requirements : protected rights

7.—(1) Unless the rules make provision such as is mentioned in sub-paragraph (2) below, the protected rights of a member are his rights to money purchase benefits under the scheme.

(2) Rules may provide that a member's protected rights are his rights under the scheme which derive from any payment of minimum contributions to the scheme, together with any rights of his to money purchase benefits which derive from protected rights under another personal pension scheme or protected rights (within the meaning of

the Social Security Pensions Act 1975) under an occupational pension scheme which have been the subject of a transfer payment and such other rights as may be prescribed.

(3) Where rules make such provision as is mentioned in sub-paragraph (2) above, they shall also make provision for the identification of the protected rights.

(4) The value of protected rights such as are mentioned in sub-paragraph (2) above—

    (a) shall be calculated in a manner no less favourable than that in which the value of any other rights of the member to money purchase benefits under the scheme are calculated ;

    (b) subject to that, shall be calculated and verified in such manner as may be prescribed.

(5) The power to make regulations conferred by sub-paragraph (4) above includes power to provide that protected rights such as are mentioned in sub-paragraph (2) above are to be calculated and verified in such manner as may be approved in particular cases—

    (a) by prescribed persons ; or

    (b) by persons with prescribed professional qualifications or experience ; or

    (c) by persons approved by the Secretary of State,

and power to provide that they shall be calculated and verified in accordance with guidance prepared by a prescribed body.

8. Rules must provide for effect to be given in a manner permitted by paragraph 9 below to the protected rights of every member and must not provide for any part of any member's protected rights to be discharged in any other way.

9.—(1) Effect may be given to protected rights—

    (a) by the provision by the scheme of a pension which—

        (i) complies with the requirements of sub-paragraph (7) below ; and

        (ii) satisfies such conditions as may be prescribed ; or

(*b*) in such circumstances and subject to such conditions as may be prescribed, by the making of a transfer payment—

    (i) to another personal pension scheme ; or

    (ii) to an occupational pension scheme,

where the scheme to which the payment is made satisfies such requirements as may be prescribed.

(2) If—

(*a*) the rules of the scheme do not provide for a pension ; or

(*b*) the member so elects,

effect may be given to protected rights by the purchase by the scheme of an annuity which—

    (i) complies with the requirements of sub-paragraphs (7) and (8) below ; and

    (ii) satisfies such conditions as may be prescribed.

(3) Effect may be given to protected rights by the provision of a lump sum if—

(*a*) the lump sum is payable on a date which is either the date on which the member attains pensionable age or such later date as has been agreed by him ; and

(*b*) the annual rate of a pension under sub-paragraph (1) above or an annuity under sub-paragraph (2) above giving effect to the protected rights and commencing on the date on which the lump sum is payable would not exceed the pre-scribed amount ; and

(*c*) the circumstances are such as may be prescribed ; and

(*d*) the amount of the lump sum is calculated in a manner satis-factory to the Occupational Pensions Board by reference to the amount of the pension or annuity.

(4) If the member has died without effect being given to protected rights under sub-paragraph (1), (2) or (3) above, effect may be given to them in such manner as may be prescribed.

(5) No transaction is to be taken to give effect to protected rights unless it falls within this paragraph.

(6) Effect need not be given to protected rights if they have been extinguished by the payment of a personal pension protected rights premium.

(7) A pension or annuity complies with this sub-paragraph if—

(*a*) it commences—

    (i) on the date on which the member attains pension-able age ; or

    (ii) on such later date as has been agreed by him,

and continues until the date of his death ;

(*b*) in a case where the member dies while it is payable to him and is survived by a widow or widower—

    (i) it is payable to the widow or widower in prescribed circumstances and for the prescribed period at an annual rate which at any given time is one-half of the rate at which it would have been payable to the member if the member had been living at that time ; or

(ii) where that annual rate would not exceed a pre-scribed amount and the circumstances are such as may be prescribed, a lump sum calculated in a manner satis-factory to the Occupational Pensions Board is provided in lieu of it.

(8) An annuity complies with the requirements of this sub-para-graph if it is provided by an insurance company which—

(a) satisfies prescribed conditions ;

(b) complies with such conditions as may be prescribed as to the calculation of annuities provided by it and as to the description of persons by or for whom they may be purchased ; and

(c) subject to sub-paragraph (9) below, has been chosen by the member.

(9) A member is only to be taken to have chosen an insurance company if he gives notice of his choice to the trustees or managers of the scheme within the prescribed period and in such manner and form as may be prescribed, and with any such supporting evidence as may be prescribed ; and, if he does not do so, the trustees or managers may themselves choose the insurance company instead.

10. The Occupational Pensions Board must be satisfied that a scheme complies with any such requirements as may be prescribed for meeting the whole or a prescribed part of any liability in respect of protected rights under the scheme which the scheme is unable to meet from its own resources—

(a) by reason of the commission by any person of a criminal offence ;

(b) in such other circumstances as may be prescribed.

11. Rules must not allow, except in such circumstances as may be prescribed, the suspension or forfeiture of a member's protected rights or of payments giving effect to them.

General

12. Nothing in this Schedule shall be taken to prejudice any requirements with which a scheme must comply if it is to qualify for tax-exemption or tax-approval.

Section 6.

SCHEDULE 2

MONEY PURCHASE CONTRACTED-OUT SCHEMES

1975 c. 60.

1. The Social Security Pensions Act 1975 shall be amended as follows.

2. In subsection (1) of section 26 (contracting-out of full contribu-tions and benefits) after the word " provides " there shall be inserted the words " or falls to be treated as providing ".

3. In section 29 (contracted-out rates of benefit) the following subsections shall be inserted after subsection (2)—

" (2A) Subject to subsection (2B) below, where for any period minimum payments have been made in respect of an earner to an occupational pension scheme which, in relation to the earner's employment, is a money purchase contracted-out scheme, then, for the purposes of this section and sections 16(2B), 28(7A) and 59(1A) of the principal Act—

> (a) the earner shall be treated, as from the date on which he reaches pensionable age, as if he were entitled to a guaranteed minimum pension at a prescribed weekly rate arising from that period in that employment ; and

> (b) in prescribed circumstances, in relation to any widow or widower of the earner—

>> (i) if the earner died after reaching pensionable age, any widow or widower of the earner shall be treated as entitled to a guaranteed minimum pension at a rate equal to one-half of the rate prescribed under paragraph (a) above ; and

>> (ii) if the earner died before reaching pensionable age, any widow or widower of the earner shall be treated as entitled to a guaranteed minimum pension at a prescribed weekly rate arising from that period.

(2B) Where the earner is a married woman or widow, subsection (2A) above shall not have effect in relation to any period during which an election that her liability in respect of primary Class 1 contributions shall be a liability to contribute at a reduced rate is operative.

(2C) The power to prescribe a rate conferred by subsection (2A)(a) above includes power to prescribe a nil rate.".

4. In section 30 (contracted-out employment)—

> (a) in subsection (1)(a), after the word " scheme " there shall be inserted the words " or his employer makes minimum payments in respect of the earner's employment to a money purchase contracted-out scheme " ;

> (b) the following subsections shall be inserted after subsection (1)—

>> " (1A) The minimum payment in respect of an earner for any tax week shall be the rebate percentage of so much of the earnings paid to or for the benefit of the earner as exceeds the lower earnings limit for the tax week but does not exceed the upper earnings limit for it ; and in this subsection " rebate percentage " means the percentage arrived at by adding—

>>> (a) the percentage by which for the time being under section 27(2) above the contracted-out percentage of primary Class 1 contributions is less than the normal percentage ; and

D 4

(*b*) the percentage by which for the time being under that subsection the contracted-out percenage of secondary Class 1 contributions is less than the normal percentage.

(1B) The references to the upper and lower earnings limits in subsection (1A) above are references, in the case of an earner who is paid otherwise than weekly, to their prescribed equivalents under section 4(2) and (6) of the principal Act.

(1C) Regulations may make provision—

(*a*) for the manner in which, and time at which or period within which, minimum payments are to be made ;

(*b*) for the recovery by employers of amounts in respect of the whole or part of minimum payments by deduction from earnings ;

(*c*) for calculating the amounts payable according to a scale prepared from time to time by the Secretary of State or otherwise adjusting them so as to avoid fractional amounts or otherwise facilitate computation ;

(*d*) for requiring that the liability in respect of a payment made in a tax week, in so far as the liability depends on any conditions as to a person's age on retirement, shall be determined as at the beginning of the week or as at the end of it :

(*e*) for securing that liability is not avoided or reduced by a person following in the payment of earnings any practice which is abnormal for the employment in respect of which the earnings are paid ;

(*f*) without prejudice to sub-paragraph (*e*) above, for enabling the Secretary of State, where he is satisfied as to the existence of any practice in respect of the payment of earnings whereby the incidence of minimum payments is avoided or reduced by means of irregular or unequal payments of earnings, to give directions for securing that minimum payments are payable as if that practice were not followed ;

(*g*) for the intervals at which, for the purposes of minimum payments, payments of earnings are to be treated as made ; and

(*h*) for this section to have effect, in prescribed cases, as if for any reference to a tax week there were substituted a reference to a prescribed period.".

5. In section 32 (contracted-out schemes)—

(*a*) in subsection (2), the words " or it satisfies subsection (2A) below." shall be inserted after paragraph (*b*) (but not as part of it) ;

(b) the following subsections shall be inserted after that sub-   Sch. 2
section—

" (2A) An occupational pension scheme satisfies this subsection only if—

   (a) the requirements imposed by or by virtue of Schedule 1
       to the Social Security Act 1986, modified under sub-
       section (2B) below, are satisfied in its case ;

   (b) it complies with section 40(1) below ; and

   (c) the rules of the scheme applying to protected rights
       are framed so as to comply with the requirements
       of any regulations prescribing the form and content
       of rules of contracted-out schemes and with such
       other requirements as to form and content (not incon-
       sistent with regulations) as may be imposed by the
       Occupational Pensions Board as a condition of con-
       tracting-out, either generally or in relation to a par-
       ticular scheme.

(2B) The modifications of Schedule 1 are—

   (a) that for the references to a personal pension scheme there
       shall be substituted references to an occupational pen-
       sion scheme ;

   (b) that for the references in paragraph 5 to minimum con-
       tributions there shall be substituted references to mini-
       mum payments and any payments by the Secretary of
       State under section 7 of the Social Security Act 1986 ;

   (c) that for paragraph 7(2) there shall be substituted—

       " (2) The rules of the scheme may provide that a
       member's protected rights are his rights under the
       scheme which derive from the payment of minimum
       payments (within the meaning of the Social Security 1975 c. 60.
       Pensions Act 1975) together with any payments by
       the Secretary of State to the scheme under section 7
       of this Act in respect of the member and any rights
       of the member to money purchase benefits which
       derive from protected rights (within the meaning of
       the Social Security Pensions Act 1975) under an-
       other occupational pension scheme or protected
       rights under a personal pension scheme which have
       been the subject of a transfer payment and such
       other rights as may be prescribed. ";

   (d) that in paragraph 9—

       (i) for the reference to an occupational pension scheme
       there shall be substituted a reference to a personal pen-
       sion scheme ; and

       (ii) for the reference to a personal pension protected
       rights premium there shall be substituted a reference to
       a contracted-out protected rights premium ; and

   (e) that paragraph 10 shall not apply to public service pen-
       sion schemes.

(2C) A contracting-out certificate shall state whether the scheme is contracted-out by virtue of subsection (2) or subsection (2A) above; and where a scheme satisfies both of those subsections the employers, in their application for a certificate, shall specify one of the subsections as the subsection by virtue of which they desire the scheme to be contracted-out.

(2D) A scheme which has been contracted-out by virtue of one of those subsections may not become contracted-out by reason of the other, except in prescribed circumstances.".

6.—(1) The words "which is not a money purchase contracted-out scheme" shall be inserted after the words "occupational pension scheme" in—

(*a*) section 33(1);

(*b*) section 36(1);

(*c*) section 40(3) and (4);

(*d*) section 41A(1);

(*e*) section 42(1);

(*f*) section 44(1);

(*g*) section 44A(1);

(*h*) section 45(1);

(*j*) section 51;

(*k*) paragraph 4(1) and (2) of Schedule 2.

(2) If section 9 above comes into force after this paragraph, the amendment to section 36(1) made by sub-paragraph (1) above shall be made in the subsection both as amended by section 9 above and as unamended.

(3) The words "or a money purchase contracted-out scheme" shall be inserted after the words "public service pension scheme" in—

(*a*) section 40(2);

(*b*) section 41(1);

(*c*) section 41E(1).

7. The following section shall be inserted after section 44—

" Money purchase schemes: contracted-out protected rights premium.

44ZA.—(1) In the case of a scheme which is or has been a money purchase contracted-out scheme the Occupational Pensions Board may, for the event of, or in connection with, its ceasing to be contracted-out, approve any arrangements made or to be made in relation to the scheme, or for its purposes, for the preservation or transfer of protected rights under the scheme.

(2) If the scheme ceases to be a contracted-out scheme (whether by being wound up or otherwise) and the Occupational Pensions Board either—

(*a*) have withdrawn their approval of previously approved arrangements relating to it ; or

(*b*) have declined to approve arrangements relating to it,

the Board may issue a certificate to that effect.

(3) A certificate issued under subsection (2)(*a*) or (*b*) above shall be cancelled by the Board if they subsequently approve the arrangements.

(4) If the scheme ceases to be a contracted-out scheme (whether by being wound up or otherwise), a state scheme premium shall be payable, except in prescribed circumstances,—

(*a*) in respect of each earner whose protected rights under the scheme are not subject to approved arrangements and have not been disposed of so as to discharge the trustees or managers of the scheme under section 52C of or paragraph 16 of Schedule 1A to this Act ; and

(*b*) in respect of each person who has become entitled to receive a pension under the scheme giving effect to protected rights which are not subject to approved arrangements.

(5) A premium under subsection (4) above may be referred to as a " contracted-out protected rights premium ".

(6) A contracted-out protected rights premium shall be paid by the prescribed person, within the prescribed period, to the Secretary of State.

(7) The amount of a contracted-out protected rights premium payable in respect of any person shall be the cash equivalent of the protected rights in question, calculated and verified in the prescribed manner.

(8) Where a contracted-out protected rights premium is paid in respect of a person—

(*a*) the rights whose cash equivalent is included in the premium shall be extinguished ; and

(*b*) section 29(2) and (2A) above and section 4 of the Social Security Act 1986 shall have effect in relation to that person and a widow or widower of that person as if any guaranteed minimum pension to which that person or any such widow or widower is treated as entitled under those provisions and which derives from the minimum payments, minimum contributions (within the meaning of the Social Security Act 1986) or transfer payment or payments from which those rights derive were reduced by the appropriate percentage.

(9) In subsection (8) above " the appropriate percentage " means, subject to the following provisions of this section,

$$\frac{X}{Y} \times 100,$$

where—

    (a) X = the amount of the premium together with, if the person in respect of whom it falls to be paid gives notice to the prescribed person within the prescribed period—

        (i) the cash equivalent, calculated and verified in the prescribed manner, and paid to the Secretary of State within the prescribed period, of any other rights which he has under the scheme and specifies in the notice ; and

        (ii) the amount of any voluntary contribution paid to the Secretary of State within the prescribed period by, or in respect of, the person concerned ; and

    (b) Y = the cost of providing any guaranteed minimum pension such as is mentioned in subsection (8) above.

(10) If the appropriate percentage, as calculated under subsection (9) above would fall between two whole numbers, it is to be taken to be the lower number.

(11) If it would be over 100, it is to be taken to be 100.

(12) The remainder after the reduction for which subsection (8) above provides—

    (a) if it would contain a fraction of 1p, is to be treated as the nearest lower whole number of pence ; and

    (b) if it would be less than a prescribed amount, is to be treated as nil.

(13) The power to make regulations conferred by subsections (7) and (9) above includes power to provide that cash equivalents are to be calculated and verified in such manner as may be approved in particular cases—

    (a) by prescribed persons ;

    (b) by persons with prescribed professional qualifications or experience ; or

    (c) by persons approved by the Secretary of State,

and power to provide that they shall be calculated and verified in accordance with guidance prepared by a prescribed body.

(14) The cost of providing the appropriate percentage of the guaranteed minimum pension shall be certified by the Secretary of State, and in calculating and certifying it the Secretary of State—

> (*a*) shall apply whichever of the prescribed actuarial tables (as in force at the time when the scheme ceases to be appropriate) is applicable in accordance with the regulations prescribing the tables ; and
>
> (*b*) may make such adjustments as he thinks necessary for avoiding fractional amounts.".

8. In section 48 (guaranteed minimum pensions to be inalienable)—

> (*a*) in subsection (1)—
>
> > (i) after the word " scheme ", in the first place where it occurs, there shall be inserted the words " or to payments giving effect to protected rights under such a scheme " ; and
> >
> > (ii) after the word " pension ", where it occurs in paragraphs (*a*) and (*b*), there shall be inserted the words " or those payments " ; and
>
> (*b*) in subsection (3), for the words from " any ", in the first place where it occurs, to " not " there shall be substituted the words " nothing whose assignment is or would be made void by that subsection shall "

9. In section 49 (supervision of schemes which have ceased to be contracted-out)—

> (*a*) the following paragraph shall be substituted for subsection (1)(*b*)—
>
> > " (*b*) there has not been a payment—
> >
> > > (i) of a premium under section 44 above in respect of each person entitled to receive, or having accrued rights to, guaranteed minimum pensions under the scheme ; or
> > >
> > > (ii) of a premium under section 44ZA above in respect of each person who has protected rights under it or is entitled to any benefit giving effect to protected rights under it ; " ;
>
> (*b*) in subsection (2)(*a*), after the word " above " there shall be inserted the words " or, by virtue of subsections (2A) and (2B) of section 32 above, paragraph 10(1) of Schedule 1 to the Social Security Act 1986 "; and
>
> (*c*) in subsection (5), " 32 " shall be substituted for " 33 ".

10. At the end of subsection (3) of section 50 (alteration of rules of contracted-out schemes) there shall be added the words " or any person has protected rights under it or is entitled to any benefit giving effect to protected rights under it ".

11. In section 66(1) (interpretation)—

(*a*) the following definition shall be inserted before the definition of " guaranteed minimum pension "—

" " average salary benefits " means benefits the rate or amount of which is calculated by reference to a member's average salary over the period of service on which the benefits are based ; " ;

(*b*) the following definitions shall be inserted after the definition of " long-term benefit "—

" " minimum payments " shall be construed in accordance with section 30 above ;

" money purchase benefits " in relation to an occupational pension scheme, means benefits the rate or amount of which is calculated by reference to a payment or payments made by a member of the scheme or by any other person in respect of a member, other than average salary benefits ;

" money purchase contracted-out scheme " means an occupational pension scheme which is contracted-out by virtue of satisfying section 32(2A) above ; " ;

(*c*) the following definition shall be inserted after the definition of " the principal Act "—

" " protected rights " has the meaning given by Schedule 1 to the Social Security Act 1986 with the substitution made by section 32(2B) above.".

12. In paragraph 2 of Schedule 3 (priority in bankruptcy etc).—

(*a*) the following sub-paragraph shall be inserted after sub-paragraph (1)—

" (1A) This Schedule applies to any sum owed on account of an employer's minimum payments to a contracted-out scheme falling to be made in the period of twelve months immediately preceding the relevant date." ; and

(*b*) in sub-paragraph (2)—

(i) the words " or payments " shall be inserted after the word " contributions " ; and

(ii) the words " or (1A) " shall be inserted after the words " sub-paragraph (1) ".

SCHEDULE 3

Industrial Injuries and Diseases

Social Security Act 1975 (c. 14)

1. The Social Security Act 1975 shall have effect as provided by this Schedule.

2. The following subsection shall be substituted for section 50(1)—

" (1) Subject to the provisions of this Act, industrial injuries benefit shall be payable where an employed earner suffers personal injury caused after 4th July 1948 by accident arising out of and in the course of his employment, being employed earner's employment.".

3.—(1) In subsection (1) of section 57 (disablement benefit) " 14 per cent." shall be substituted for " 1 per cent.".

(2) The following subsections shall be inserted after that sub-section—

"(1A) In the determination of the extent of an employed earner's disablement for the purposes of this section there may be added to the percentage of the disablement resulting from the relevant accident the assessed percentage of any present dis-ablement of his resulting from any other accident after 4th July 1948 which arose out of and in the course of his employment, being employed earner's employment, and in respect of which a disablement gratuity was not paid to him under this Act after a final assessment of his disablement.

(1B) Subject to subsection (1C) below, where the assessment of disablement is a percentage between 20 and 100 which is not a multiple of 10, it shall be treated—

(a) if it is a multiple of 5, as being the next higher per-centage which is a multiple of 10 ; and

(b) if it is not a multiple of 5, as being the nearest per-centage which is a multiple of 10,

and where it is a percentage of 14 or more but less than 20 it shall be treated as a percentage of 20.

(1C) Where subsection (1A) above applies, subsection (1B) above shall have effect in relation to the aggregate percentage and not in relation to any percentage forming part of the aggregate.".

(3) Subsection (5) of that section shall cease to have effect except in relation to cases where the claim for benefit was made before this paragraph comes into force.

(4) Subsection (6) shall have effect, except in relation to such cases, as if the words " Where disablement benefit is payable for a period, it shall be paid " were substituted for the words from the beginning to " payable ".

4. Sections 58 and 59 and 64 to 66 (unemployability supplement) shall cease to have effect, except in relation to beneficiaries in re-ceipt of unemployability supplement immediately before this para-graph comes into force.

5.—(1) The following section shall be inserted after section 59—

"Reduced earnings allowance.   59A.—(1) Subject to the provisions of this Part of this Act, an employed earner shall be entitled to reduced earnings allowance if—

(a) he is entitled to a disablement pension or would be so entitled if that pension were payable where disablement is assessed at not less than 1 per cent. ;

SCH. 3

(*b*) as a result of the relevant loss of faculty, he is either—

>> (i) incapable, and likely to remain permanently incapable, of following his regular occupation ; and

>> (ii) incapable of following employment of an equivalent standard which is suitable in his case,

> or is, and has at all times since the end of the period of 90 days referred to in section 57(4) above been, incapable of following that occupation or any such employment.

(2) The Secretary of State may by regulations provide that in prescribed circumstances employed earner's employment in which a claimant was engaged when the relevant accident took place but which was not his regular occupation is to be treated as if it had been his regular occupation.

(3) In subsection (1) above—

> (*a*) references to a person's regular occupation are to be taken as not including any subsidiary occupation, except to the extent that they fall to be treated as including such an occupation by virtue of regulations under subsection (2) above ; and

> (*b*) employment of an equivalent standard is to be taken as not including employment other than employed earner's employment ;

and in assessing the standard of remuneration in any employment, including a person's regular occupation, regard is to be had to his reasonable prospect of advancement.

(4) For the purposes of this section a person's regular occupation is to be treated as extending to and including employment in the capacities to which the persons in that occupation (or a class or description of them to which he belonged at the time of the relevant accident) are in the normal course advanced, and to which, if he had continued to follow that occupation without having suffered the relevant loss of faculty, he would have had at least the normal prospects of advancement ; and so long as he is, as a result of the relevant loss of faculty, deprived in whole or in part of those prospects, he is to be treated as incapable of following that occupation.

(5) Regulations may for the purposes of this section provide that a person is not to be treated as capable of following an occupation or employment merely because of his working thereat during a period of trial or for purposes of rehabilitation or training or in other prescribed circumstances.

(6) Reduced earnings allowance shall be awarded—

   (*a*) for such period as may be determined at the time of the award ; and

   (*b*) if at the end of that period the beneficiary submits a fresh claim for the allowance, for such further period as may be determined.

(7) The award may not be for a period longer than the period to be taken into account under paragraph 4 or 4A of Schedule 8 to this Act.

(8) Reduced earnings allowance shall be payable at a rate determined by reference to the beneficiary's probable standard of remuneration during the period for which it is granted in any employed earner's employments which are suitable in his case and which he is likely to be capable of following as compared with that in the relevant occupation, but in no case at a rate higher than 40 per cent. of the maximum rate of a disablement pension or at a rate such that the aggregate of disablement pension and reduced earnings allowance awarded to the beneficiary exceeds 140 per cent. of the maximum rate of a disablement pension.

(9) In subsection (8) above " the relevant occupation " means—

   (*a*) in relation to a person who is entitled to reduced earnings allowance by virtue of regulations under subsection (2) above, the occupation in which he was engaged when the relevant accident took place ; and

   (*b*) in relation to any other person who is entitled to reduced earnings allowance, his regular occupation within the meaning of subsection (1) above.

(10) On any award except the first the probable standard of his remuneration shall be determined in such manner as may be prescribed ; and, without prejudice to the generality of this subsection, regulations may provide in prescribed circumstances for the probable standard of remuneration to be determined by reference—

   (*a*) to the standard determined at the time of the last previous award of reduced earnings allowance ; and

   (*b*) to scales or indices of earnings in a particular industry or description of industries or any other data relating to such earnings.

(11) A person who—

   (*a*) attains pensionable age after this section comes into force ; and

   (*b*) has retired from regular employment before that day ; and

(c) was entitled to reduced earnings allowance on the day immediately before he retired from regular employment,

shall be treated as entitled as from the day on which he retires from regular employment to reduced earnings allowance at a rate not higher at any time than that at which the allowance was payable to him immediately before he retired from regular employment.".

(2) Section 60 (increase of disablement pension for special hardship) shall cease to have effect.

(3) A person who—

(a) is over pensionable age on the day on which this paragraph comes into force ; and

(b) has retired from regular employment before that day ; and

(c) was entitled on the day immediately before that day to an increase under section 60,

shall be treated as entitled as from the day on which this paragraph comes into force to reduced earnings allowance at a rate not higher at any time than that at which the increase was payable to him immediately before that day.

(4) Where for any period commencing before 6th April 1987 a person is entitled both to reduced earnings allowance under section 59A and to an additional pension of a long-term benefit or, if the long-term benefit is invalidity pension, to either an invalidity allowance or an additional pension, or both, his reduced earnings allowance shall be reduced in respect of any part of the period falling on or after 6th April 1987 by the amount of any increase in the additional pension or invalidity allowance as the result of an order under section 63 above taking effect on or after that date.

(5) Where for any period commencing on or after 6th April 1987 a person is entitled as mentioned in sub-paragraph (4) above, his reduced earnings allowance shall be reduced by the amount of any additional pension or invalidity allowance to which he is entitled.

(6) Where a reduction falls to be made under sub-paragraph (4) or (5) above, the person to whom it falls to be made shall be entitled to reduced earnings allowance only if there is a balance after the reduction and, if there is such a balance, of an amount equal to it.

(7) Where the weekly rate of a benefit is reduced under section 29 of the Social Security Pensions Act 1975, there shall be subtracted from the amount which would otherwise fall to be deducted under sub-paragraph (4) or (5) above an amount equal to the reduction under that section.

(8) In the preceding sub-paragraphs references to an additional pension are references to that pension after any increase under section 9(3) of the Social Security Pensions Act 1975 but without any increase under Schedule 1, paragraphs 1 and 2, to that Act.

6. The following subsections shall be inserted after subsection (2) of section 61 (constant attendance allowance)—

Sch. 3

" (3) The Secretary of State may by regulations direct that any provision of section 35 above shall have effect, with or without modifications, in relation to increases of pension under this section.

(4) In subsection (3) above " modifications " includes additions and omissions.".

7. Section 62 (increase during hospital treatment) shall cease to have effect, except in relation to a period during which a person is receiving medical treatment as an in-patient in a hospital or similar institution and which—

(*a*) commenced before the coming into force of this paragraph ; or

(*b*) commenced after it but within a period of 28 days from the end of the period during which he last received an increase of benefit under that section in respect of such treatment for the relevant injury or loss of faculty.

8. The following provisions (which all relate to industrial death benefit)—

(*a*) sections 67 and 68 ;

(*b*) sections 70 to 75 ; and

(*c*) Schedule 9,

shall cease to have effect.

9.—(1) This paragraph shall have effect in relation to widows who on the day before paragraph 8 above comes into force are entitled to death benefit under section 67.

(2) A widow who is entitled to a pension at the initial rate specified in Schedule 4, Part V, paragraph 13(*a*) shall be treated as satisfying the conditions of entitlement to a widow's allowance specified in subsection (1) of section 24 and her entitlement to the allowance under that section shall, subject to the proviso to subsection (2) of that section, continue for so long as she would have been entitled to a pension under section 67 at the initial rate.

(3) A widow who—

(*a*) is not entitled to a pension at the initial rate but has one or more dependent children ; or

(*b*) is pregnant on the day before paragraph 8 above comes into force,

shall be treated as satisfying the conditions of entitlement to a widowed mother's allowance under section 25 and her entitlement to the allowance shall, subject to the proviso to subsection (3) of that section, continue for so long as she satisfies either of the conditions specified in paragraph (*a*) or (*b*) of subsection (1) of that section.

(4) A widow who—

   (*a*) is under 60 ; and

   (*b*) has no dependent child ; and

   (*c*) does not fall to be treated as entitled to a widow's allowance or a widowed mother's allowance,

shall be treated as satisfying the conditions of entitlement to a widow's pension under section 26 and the pension shall be payable for any period during which she satisfies the provisions of subsection (3) of that section.

(5) Subject to sub-paragraph (6) below, the rate of a widow's pension under sub-paragraph (4) above shall be—

   (*a*) in the case of a widow who was entitled to an allowance under section 70 after her husband died, but has ceased to be so entitled, the rate for a widow of the age she was when she so ceased ;

   (*b*) in the case of a widow who was not so entitled, the rate for a widow of the age she was when her late husband died,

and for the purposes of this subsection a woman who was under the age of 40 at the relevant time shall be treated as having been of the age of 40 at that time.

(6) The rate of pension for a widow who is entitled under section 68(2) to a pension at the higher permanent rate specified in Schedule 4, Part V, paragraph 13(*b*), shall be the rate specified in section 13 of the Social Security Pensions Act 1975 and shall be that rate notwithstanding anything in subsection (3) of that section.

1975 c. 60.

(7) Regulations may provide that a widow who on the day before paragraph 8 above comes into force is entitled to death benefit under section 67 shall be entitled to a prescribed benefit at a prescribed rate.

(8) In this paragraph " dependent child " means a child in respect of whom the widow is entitled to child benefit if one of the conditions specified in section 43(1) is for the time being satisfied with respect to the child and the child is either—

   (*a*) a son or daughter of the widow and her late husband ; or

   (*b*) a child in respect of whom her late husband was immediately before his death entitled to child benefit ; or

   (*c*) if the widow and her late husband were residing together immediately before his death, a child in respect of whom she was then entitled to child benefit.

10. In any case where—

   (*a*) an employed earner who is married dies as a result—

      (i) of a personal injury of a kind mentioned in section 50(1) ; or

      (ii) of a disease or injury such as is mentioned in section 76(1) ;

(*b*) the contribution conditions are not wholly satisfied in respect of him ;

those conditions shall be taken to be satisfied for the purposes of his widow's entitlement to—

(i) a widow's allowance or widow's payment ;

(ii) a widowed mother's allowance ;

(iii) a widow's pension ; or

(iv) a Category B retirement pension at the same weekly rate as her widow's pension.

11. Section 69 (widower's death benefit) shall cease to have effect, except in relation to widowers in receipt of death benefit immediately before this paragraph comes into force.

12. The Secretary of State may by regulations provide for the payment of prescribed amounts in prescribed circumstances to persons who immediately before the repeal of sections 71 to 73 were entitled to any benefit by virtue of any of those sections, but in determining the amount which is to be payable in any case or class of cases the Secretary of State may take into account—

(*a*) the extent to which the weekly rate of industrial death benefit has been modified in that case or class of cases by virtue of section 74 ;

(*b*) the age of the beneficiary and of any person or persons formerly maintained by the deceased ; and

(*c*) the length of time that entitlement to the benefit would have been likely to continue if those sections had not been repealed.

13. In section 77 (regulations as to industrial diseases) the following subsections shall be inserted after subsection (3)—

" (4) The regulations may also provide—

(*a*) that in the determination of the extent of an employed earner's disablement resulting from a prescribed disease or injury there may be added to the percentage of that disablement the assessed percentage of any present disablement of his resulting from—

(i) any accident after 4th July 1948 arising out of and in the course of his employment, being employed earner's employment ;

(ii) any other prescribed disease or injury due to the nature of that employment and developed after 4th July 1948,

and in respect of which a disablement gratuity was not paid to him under this Act after a final assessment of his disablement ; and

(*b*) that in the determination of the extent of an employed earner's disablement for the purposes of section 57 above there may be added to the percentage of disablement resulting from the relevant accident the assessed percentage of any present disablement of his resulting from any prescribed disease or injury due to the nature of his employment and developed after 4th July 1948 and in respect of which a disablement gratuity was not paid to him under this Act after a final assessment of his disablement.

(5) Where the regulations make provision such as is mentioned in subsection (4) above and also make provision corresponding to subsection (1B) of section 57 above, they may also make provision to the effect that the corresponding provisions shall have effect in relation to the aggregate percentage and not in relation to any percentage forming part of the aggregate.".

14. In section 108 (disablement questions)—

(a) in subsection (1) the following words shall be added at the end, but not as part of paragraph (b)—

"but questions relating to the aggregation of percentages of disablement resulting from different accidents are not disablement questions." ; and

(b) the following subsection shall be inserted after subsection (4)—

" (4A) In the case of a claimant for disablement benefit the adjudication officer may refer to one or more adjudicating medical practitioners for determination any question as to the extent of any present disablement of his resulting from an accident other than the accident which is the basis of the claim.".

15. In Schedule 8 (assessment of extent of disablement)—

(a) paragraph 4 shall be renumbered as sub-paragraph (1) of that paragraph ; and

(b) the following sub-paragraph shall be inserted after that sub-paragraph—

" (2) Where—

(a) the assessed extent of a claimant's disablement amounts to 13 per cent. or less ;

(b) it seems likely that the assessed extent of a claimant's disablement will be aggregated with the assessed extent of any present disablement of his and the likely aggregate amounts to 13 per cent. or less,

the period to be taken into account by the assessment of the disablement shall not end earlier than any date by which it seems likely that the extent of the disablement or the aggregate will be at least 1 per cent.".

Industrial Injuries and Diseases (Old Cases) Act 1975 (c. 16)

16. For the purposes of section 159 and of section 7 of the Industrial Injuries and Diseases (Old Cases) Act 1975 paragraph 4 of this Schedule shall be deemed not to have been enacted.

Pneumoconiosis etc. (Workers' Compensation) Act 1979 (c. 41)   Sch. 3

17.—(1) Section 2 of the Pneumoconiosis etc. (Workers' Compensation) Act 1979 (conditions of entitlement to lump sum payments) shall be amended as follows.

(2) At the end of subsection (1)(*a*) there shall be added the words " or, subject to subsection (3A) below, would be payable to him in respect of it but for his disablement amounting to less than the appropriate percentage ".

(3) At the end of subsection (2)(*b*) there shall be added the words " or, subject to subsection (3A) below, would have been so payable to him—

(i) but for his disablement amounting to less than the appropriate percentage ; or

(ii) but for his not having claimed the benefit ; or

(iii) but for his having died before he had suffered from the disease for the appropriate period ".

(4) In subsection (3) the following definitions shall be inserted before the definition of " death benefit "—

" the appropriate percentage " means, in the case of any disease, the percentage specified in subsection (1) of section 57 of the Social Security Act 1975 or, if regulations have 1975 c. 14. been made under section 77 of that Act specifying a different percentage in relation to that disease, the percentage specified in the regulations ;

" the appropriate period " means, in the case of any disease, the period specified in subsection (4) of the said section 57 or, if regulations have been made under the said section 77 specifying a different period in relation to that disease, the period specified in the regulations ; ".

(5) The following subsection shall be inserted after that subsection—

" (3A) No amount is payable under this Act in respect of disablement amounting to less than 1 per cent.".

SCHEDULE 4

    Section 49.

Statutory Maternity Pay etc.

Part I

Provisions Supplementary to
Part V

Recovery of amounts paid by way of statutory maternity pay

1. Regulations shall make provision—

(*a*) entitling, except in prescribed circumstances, any person who has made a payment of statutory maternity pay to recover the amount so paid by making one or more deductions from his contributions payments ; and

(b) for the payment, in prescribed circumstances, by the Secretary of State or by the Commissioners of Inland Revenue on behalf of the Secretary of State, of sums to persons who are unable so to recover the whole, or any part, of any payments of statutory maternity pay which they have made ;

(c) giving any person who has made a payment of statutory maternity pay a right, except in prescribed circumstances, to an amount, determined in such manner as may be prescribed—

(i) by reference to secondary Class 1 contributions paid in respect of statutory maternity pay ; or

(ii) by reference to secondary Class 1 contributions paid in respect of statutory sick pay ; or

(iii) by reference to the aggregate of secondary Class 1 contributions paid in respect of statutory maternity pay and secondary Class 1 contributions paid in respect of statutory sick pay ;

(d) providing for the recovery, in prescribed circumstances, of the whole or any part of any such amount from contributions payments ;

(e) for the payment, in prescribed circumstances, by the Secretary of State or by the Commissioners of Inland Revenue on behalf of the Secretary of State, of the whole or any part of any such amount.

2. Regulations under paragraph 1 above may, in particular provide for any deduction made in accordance with the regulations to be disregarded for prescribed purposes.

3. The power to make regulations conferred by paragraph 5 of Schedule 1 to the Social Security Act 1975 (power to combine collection of contributions with collection of income tax) shall include power to make such provision as the Secretary of State considers expedient in consequence of any provision made by or under this Schedule.

4. Provision made in regulations under paragraph 5 of Schedule 1, by virtue of paragraph 3 above, may in particular require the inclusion—

(a) in returns, certificates and other documents ; or

(b) in any other form of record ;

which the regulations require to be kept or produced or to which those regulations otherwise apply, of such particulars relating to statutory maternity pay or deductions or payments made by virtue of paragraph 1 above as may be prescribed by those regulations.

5. Where, in accordance with any provision of regulations made under this Schedule, an amount has been deducted from an employer's contributions payments, the amount so deducted shall (except in such cases as may be prescribed) be treated for the purposes of

any provision made by or under any enactment in relation to primary or secondary Class 1 contributions as having been—

(*a*) paid (on such date as may be determined in accordance with the regulations) ; and

(*b*) received by the Secretary of State,

towards discharging the employer's liability in respect of such contributions.

Provision of information by women and their employers and/or former employers

6. A woman shall provide the person who is liable to pay her statutory maternity pay—

(*a*) with evidence as to her pregnancy and the expected date of confinement in such form and at such time as may be prescribed ; and

(*b*) where she commences work after her confinement but within the maternity pay period, with such additional information as may be prescribed.

7. Where a woman asks an employer or former employer of hers to provide her with a written statement, in respect of a period before the request is made, of one or more of the following—

(*a*) the weeks within that period which he regards as weeks in respect of which he is liable to pay statutory maternity pay to the woman ;

(*b*) the reasons why he does not so regard the other weeks in that period ; and

(*c*) his opinion as to the amount of statutory maternity pay to which the woman is entitled in respect of each of the weeks in respect of which he regards himself as liable to make a payment,

the employer or former employer shall, to the extent to which the request was reasonable, comply with it within a reasonable time.

8. Regulations—

(*a*) may require employers to maintain such records in connection with statutory maternity pay as may be prescribed ;

(*b*) may provide for—

(i) any woman claiming to be entitled to statutory maternity pay ; or

(ii) any other person who is a party to proceedings arising under this Act relating to statutory maternity pay,

to furnish to the Secretary of State, within a prescribed period, any information required for the determination of any question arising in connection therewith ; and

(*c*) may require persons who have made payments of statutory maternity pay to furnish to the Secretary of State such documents and information, at such time, as may be prescribed.

Provision of information by Secretary of State

9. Where the Secretary of State considers that it is reasonable for information held by him to be disclosed to a person liable to

Sch. 4   make payments of statutory maternity pay for the purpose of enabling that person to determine—

     (*a*) whether a maternity pay period exists in relation to a woman who is or has been an employee of his ; and

     (*b*) if it does, the date of its commencement and the weeks in it in respect of which he may be liable to pay statutory maternity pay,

he may disclose the information to that person.

Statutory maternity pay to count as remuneration for purposes of Social Security Act 1975

1975 c. 14.   10. For the purposes of section 3 of the Social Security Act 1975 (meaning of "earnings"), any sums paid to, or for the benefit of, a woman in satisfaction (whether in whole or in part) of any entitlement of hers to statutory maternity pay shall be treated as remuneration derived from employed earner's employment.

Relationship with benefits and other payments etc.

11. Any day which falls within the maternity pay period shall not be treated for the purposes of the Social Security Act 1975 or the 1975 c. 60.   Social Security Pensions Act 1975 as a day of unemployment or of incapacity for work for the purpose of determining whether it forms part of a period of interruption of employment.

12.—(1) Subject to sub-paragraphs (2) and (3) below, any entitlement to statutory maternity pay shall not affect any right of a woman in relation to remuneration under any contract of service(" contractual remuneration ").

(2) Subject to sub-paragraph (3) below—

     (*a*) any contractual remuneration paid to a woman by an employer of hers in respect of a week in the maternity pay period shall go towards discharging any liability of that employer to pay statutory maternity pay to her in respect of that week ; and

     (*b*) any statutory maternity pay paid by an employer to a woman who is an employee of his in respect of a week in the maternity pay period shall go towards discharging any liability of that employer to pay contractual remuneration to her in respect of that week.

(3) Regulations may make provision as to payments which are, and those which are not, to be treated as contractual remuneration for the purposes of sub-paragraphs (1) and (2) above.

Part II

Amendments of Social Security Act 1975

13. For sections 22 and 23 there shall be substituted—

" State maternity allowance.   22.—(1) A woman shall be entitled to a maternity allowance at the weekly rate specified in relation thereto in Schedule 4, Part I, paragraph 4, if—

     (*a*) she satisfies the condition specified in section 46(2)(*c*) of the Social Security Act 1986 ; and (*b*) she has been engaged in employment as an employed or self-employed earner for at least 26 weeks in the 52 weeks immediately preceding the 14th week before the expected week of confinement ; and

(*c*) she satisfies the contribution condition for a maternity allowance specified in Schedule 3, Part I, paragraph 3 ; and

(*d*) she is not entitled to statutory maternity pay for the same week in respect of the same pregnancy.

(2) Subject to the following provisions of this section, a maternity allowance shall be payable for the period ("the maternity allowance period") which, if she were entitled to statutory maternity pay, would be the maternity pay period under section 47 of the Social Security Act 1986.

(3) Regulations may provide—

(*a*) for disqualifying a woman for receiving a maternity allowance if—

(i) during the maternity allowance period she does any work in employment as an employed or self-employed earner or fails without good cause to observe any prescribed rules of behaviour ; or

(ii) at any time before she is confined she fails without good cause to attend for, or submit herself to, any medical examination required in accordance with the regulations ;

(*b*) that this section and Schedule 3, Part I, paragraph 3 shall have effect subject to prescribed modifications in relation to cases in which a woman has been confined and—

(i) has not made a claim for a maternity allowance in expectation of that confinement (other than a claim which has been disallowed) ; or

(ii) has made a claim for maternity allowance in expectation of that confinement (other than a claim which has been disallowed), but she was confined more than 11 weeks before the expected week of confinement.

(4) Any day which falls within the maternity allowance period shall be treated for the purposes of this Part of this Act as a day of incapacity for work.

(5) Where for any purpose of this Part of this Act or of regulations it is necessary to calculate the daily rate of a maternity allowance—

(*a*) Sunday or such other day in each week as may be prescribed shall be disregarded ; and (*b*) the amount payable by way of that allowance for any other day shall be taken as ⅙th of the weekly rate of the allowance.

    (6) In this section " confinement " and " confined " are to be construed in accordance with section 50 of the Social Security Act 1986.

    (7) The fact that the mother of a child is being paid maternity allowance shall not be taken into consideration by any court in deciding whether to order payment of expenses incidental to the birth of the child.".

14. The following paragraph shall be substituted for paragraph 3 of Part I of Schedule 3—

    " 3. The contribution condition for a maternity allowance is—

        (*a*) that the claimant must in respect of at least 26 weeks in the 52 weeks immediately preceding the 14th week before the expected week of confinement have actually paid contributions of a relevant class ; and

        (*b*) in the case of Class 1 contributions, that they were not secondary contributions and were not ˙paid at the reduced rate.".

Part III

Abolition of Maternity Pay and Winding-up of Maternity Pay Fund

1978 c. 44.

15. The provisions of Part III of the Employment Protection (Consolidation) Act 1978 shall cease to have effect so far as they relate to maternity pay.

16. A woman who is entitled to maternity pay on the coming into force of paragraph 15 above shall continue to be so entitled notwithstanding that paragraph ; but a woman who continues to be entitled to maternity pay by virtue of this paragraph shall not be entitled to statutory maternity pay in respect of any week as respects which she is entitled to maternity pay.

17.—(1) The assets and liabilities of the Maternity Pay Fund (including, in particular, liabilities of the Secretary of State in respect of sums advanced under section 38 of the Employment Protection (Consolidation) Act 1978 or claims under section 39 or 40 of that Act) immediately before the relevant date shall become assets and liabilities of the National Insurance Fund ; and on that date the Maternity Pay Fund shall cease to exist.

    (2) Not later than such date as the Treasury may direct the Secretary of State shall prepare an account in such form as the Treasury may direct showing the state of the Maternity Pay Fund on the relevant date.

(3) The Secretary of State shall send to the Comptroller and Auditor General a copy of the account prepared under sub-paragraph (2) above ; and the Comptroller and Auditor General shall examine, certify and report on the account and lay copies of it and of his report before each House of Parliament.

(4) In this paragraph " the relevant date " means such date in the period of 12 months ending on 5th April 1988 as the Secretary of State may, with the consent of the Treasury, determine.

SCHEDULE 5

ADJUDICATION

PART I

AMENDMENT OF ENACTMENTS

Social Security Act 1973 (c. 38)

1. In section 67(2) of the Social Security Act 1973 (review of determinations by Occupational Pensions Board) the words " or was erroneous in point of law " shall be inserted at the end of paragraph (*a*).

Social Security Act 1975 (c. 14)

2. Section 95 of the Social Security Act 1975 (other questions for Secretary of State) shall cease to have effect.

3. The following subsection shall be substituted for subsection (1) of section 96 of that Act (review of certain decisions of Secretary of State)—

" (1) Subject to subsection (2) below, the Secretary of State may review any decision given by him on any question within section 93(1) above if—

(*a*) new facts have been brought to his notice ; or

(*b*) he is satisfied that the decision—

(i) was given in ignorance of some material fact ;

(ii) was based on a mistake as to some material fact ; or

(iii) was erroneous in point of law.".

4. The following subsections shall be substituted for subsection (2) of section 98 of that Act (claims and questions to be submitted to adjudication officer)—

" (2) Subsection (1) above does not apply to any question which falls to be determined otherwise than by an adjudication officer.

(2A) If—

(*a*) a person submits a question relating to the age, marriage or death of any person ; and

(*b*) it appears to the adjudication officer that the question may arise if the person who has submitted it to him submits a claim for benefit,

the adjudication officer may determine the question.".

5. The following subsection shall be substituted for subsection (2) of section 99 of that Act (decision of adjudication officer)—

" (2) Subject to section 103 below (reference of special questions), the adjudication officer may decide a claim or question himself or refer it to a social security appeal tribunal.".

6. In section 100 of that Act (appeal to social security appeal tribunal)—

(a) in subsection (1), the words " adversely to the claimant " shall be omitted ;

(b) in subsection (2), for the words from " notified " to the end there shall be substituted the words " given any such notification of a decision and of his right of appeal under this section as may be prescribed." ;

(c) for the words from the beginning of subsection (3) to the end of paragraph (b) there shall be substituted the words " Where in connection with the decision of the adjudication officer there has arisen any question which under or by virtue of this Act falls to be determined otherwise than by an adjudication officer " ;

(d) the following subsection shall be substituted for subsection (4)—

" (4) Regulations may make provision as to the manner in which, and the time within which, appeals are to be brought." ;

(e) the following subsection shall be substituted for subsection (7)—

" (7) Where an adjudication officer has determined that any amount is recoverable under or by virtue of section 27 or 53 of the Social Security Act 1986 (over payments) any person from whom he has determined that it is recoverable shall have the same right of appeal to a social security appeal tribunal as a claimant.".

7.—(1) At the end of subsection (1) of section 101 of that Act (appeal from tribunal to Commissioner) there shall be added the words " on the ground that the decision of the tribunal was erroneous in point of law.".

(2) The following paragraph shall be substituted for paragraph (d) of subsection (2) of that section—

" (d) a person from whom it is determined that any amount is recoverable under or by virtue of section 27 or 53 of the Social Security Act 1986.".

(3) The following subsections shall be substituted for subsection (5) of that section—

" (5) Where the Commissioner holds that the decision was erroneous in point of law—

(a) he shall have power—

(i) to give the decision which he considers the tribunal should have given, if he can do so without making fresh or further findings of fact ; or

(ii) if he considers it expedient, to make such findings and to give such decision as he considers appropriate in the light of them ; and

(b) in any other case he shall refer the case to a tribunal with directions for its determination.

(5A) No appeal lies under this section without the leave—

(a) of the person who was the chairman of the tribunal when the decision was given or, in a case prescribed by regulations, the leave of some other chairman of a social security appeal tribunal ; or

(b) subject to and in accordance with regulations, of a Commissioner.

(5B) Regulations may make provision as to the manner in which, and the time within which, appeals are to be brought and applications made for leave to appeal.".

8. The following subsection shall be substituted for subsection (2) of section 102 of that Act (question first arising on appeal)—

" (2) Subsection (1) above does not apply to any question which under or by virtue of this Act falls to be determined otherwise than by an adjudication officer.".

9. The following section shall be substituted for section 103 of that Act—

" Reference of special questions.

103.—(1) Subject to subsection (2) below—

(a) if on consideration of any claim or question an adjudication officer is of opinion that there arises any question which under or by virtue of this Act falls to be determined otherwise than by an adjudication officer, he shall refer the question for such determination ; and

(b) if on consideration of any claim or question a social security appeal tribunal or a Commissioner is of opinion that any such question arises, the tribunal or Commissioner shall direct it to be referred by an adjudication officer for such determination.

(2) The person or tribunal making the reference shall then deal with any other question as if the referred question had not arisen.

(3) The adjudication officer, tribunal or Commissioner may—

    (*a*) postpone the reference of, or dealing with, any question until other questions have been determined ;

    (*b*) in cases where the determination of any question disposes of a claim or any part of it make an award or decide that an award cannot be made, as to the claim or that part of it, without referring or dealing with, or before the determination of, any other question.".

10. In section 104 of that Act (review of decisions of adjudication officers, tribunals or Commissioner)—

    (*a*) the following subsection shall be substituted for subsection (1)—

        " (1) Any decision under this Act of an adjudication officer, a social security appeal tribunal or a Commissioner may be reviewed at any time by an adjudication officer, or, on a reference by an adjudication officer, by a social security appeal tribunal, if—

        (*a*) the officer or tribunal is satisfied that the decision was given in ignorance of, or was based on a mistake as to, some material fact ; or

        (*b*) there has been any relevant change of circumstances since the decision was given ; or

        (*c*) the decision was based on a decision of a question which under or by virtue of this Act falls to be determined otherwise than by an adjudication officer, and the decision of that question is revised,

        but regulations may provide that a decision may not be reviewed on the ground mentioned in paragraph (*a*) above unless the officer or tribunal is satisfied as mentioned in that paragraph by fresh evidence." ;

    (*b*) in subsection (1A), the words " in prescribed circumstances " shall cease to have effect ;

    (*c*) the following subsection shall be inserted after subsection (3)—

        " (3A) Regulations may provide for enabling or requiring, in prescribed circumstances, a review under this section notwithstanding that no application under subsection (2) has been made." ; and

    (*d*) the following subsection shall be added after subsection (4)—

        " (5) Regulations—

        (*a*) may prescribe what are, or are not, relevant changes of circumstances for the purposes of subsection (1)(*b*) above ; and (*b*) may make provision restricting the payment of any benefit, or any increase of benefit, to which a person would, but for this subsection, be entitled by reason of a review in respect of any period before the review.".

11.—(1) In section 106(1) of that Act (review of decision of Attendance Allowance Board) in paragraph (*b*) before the word " within " there shall be inserted the words " on an application made ".

(2) The following paragraph shall be inserted after that paragraph—

    " (*bb*) without an application review such a determination on any ground within the prescribed period ; ".

12. In section 107(6) of that Act (declaration that accident is an industrial accident)—

    (*a*) the words " or was not " shall be inserted after the words " accident was " ; and

    (*b*) the words " by fresh evidence " and paragraph (*b*) shall cease to have effect.

13. In section 109(3) of that Act (medical appeals and references) after the words " by a medical appeal tribunal," there shall be inserted the words " or, if the adjudication officer is of the opinion that any such decision ought to be so considered,".

14. In section 110 of that Act (review of medical decisions)—

    (*a*) in subsection (1), the words " by fresh evidence " shall cease to have effect ; and

    (*b*) the following subsections shall be inserted after that subsection—

    " (1A) Any decision under this Part of this Act of an adjudicating medical practitioner may be reviewed at any time by such a practitioner if he is satisfied that the decision was erroneous in point of law.

    (1B) Regulations may provide that a decision may not be reviewed under subsection (1) above unless the adjudicating medical practitioner is satisfied as mentioned in that subsection by fresh evidence.".

15. In section 112 of that Act (appeal etc. on question of law to Commissioner)—

    (*a*) in subsection (1), the following paragraph shall be inserted before paragraph (*a*)—

        " (*za*) an adjudication officer ; or " ; and

    (*b*) in subsection (3), for the words from " without the leave " to " and regulations " there shall be substituted—

        " without the leave—

        (*a*) of the person who was the chairman of the medical appeal tribunal when the decision was given or, in a case prescribed by regulations, the leave of some other chairman of a medical appeal tribunal ; or

E

(*b*) subject to and in accordance with regulations, of a Commissioner,

and regulations ".

16. In section 114 of that Act (regulations as to determination of questions)—

(*a*) the following subsections shall be inserted after subsection (2A)—

" (2B) Regulations under subsection (1) above may provide for the review by the Secretary of State of decisions on questions determined by him.

(2C) The Lord Chancellor may by regulations provide—

(*a*) for officers authorised—

(i) by the Lord Chancellor ; or

(ii) in Scotland, by the Secretary of State,

to determine any question which is determinable by a Commissioner and which does not involve the determination of any appeal, application for leave to appeal or reference ;

(*b*) for the procedure to be followed by any such officer in determining any such question ;

(*c*) for the manner in which determinations of such questions by such officers may be called in question.

(2D) A determination which would have the effect of preventing an appeal, application for leave to appeal or reference being determined by a Commissioner is not a determination of the appeal, application or reference for the purposes of subsection (2C) above." ; and

(*b*) subsections (3) and (4) shall cease to have effect.

17. The following subsection shall be inserted after section 166(5) of that Act (regulations)—

" (5A) Where the Lord Chancellor proposes to make regulations under this Act it shall be his duty to consult the Lord Advocate with respect to the proposal.".

18. In paragraph 2(2) of Schedule 12 to that Act (appointment of members of medical appeal tribunals) for the words " Secretary of State " there shall be substituted the word " President ".

19. In Schedule 13 to that Act (provision which may be made by procedure regulations)—

(*a*) the following paragraph shall be inserted after paragraph 1—

" 1A. Provision as to the striking out of proceedings for want of prosecution." ;

SCH. 5

(*b*) in paragraph 10, for the words from " the determination " to the end there shall be substituted the words " a determination.".

20. In Schedule 20 to that Act (glossary of expressions), for the definition of " Regulations " there shall be substituted the following definition—

" Regulations ".

In relation to regulations with respect to proceedings before the Commissioners (whether for the determination of any matter or for leave to appeal to or from the Commissioners) and to regulations under section 114(2C) above regulations made by the Lord Chancellor under this Act and in relation to other regulations, regulations made by the Secretary of State under this Act.".

PART II

QUESTIONS FOR DETERMINATION BY THE SECRETARY OF STATE

The questions referred to in section 52(2) above are—

(*a*) any question arising in connection with—

(i) minimum contributions ;

(ii) any state scheme premium under Part I of this Act ; or

(iii) payments under section 7 above,

other than a question which is required under or by virtue of this Act or the Social Security Pensions Act 1975 to be determined by the Occupational Pensions Board ;

1975 c. 60.

(*b*) any question arising under any provision of Part I of the Social Security and Housing Benefits Act 1982, or of regulations under that Part of that Act, as to—

1982 c. 24.

(i) whether a person is, or was, an employee or employer of another ;

(ii) whether an employer is entitled to make any deduction from his contributions payments in accordance with regulations under section 9 of that Act ;

(iii) whether a payment falls to be made to an employer in accordance with the regulations ;

(iv) the amount that falls to be so deducted or paid ; or

(v) whether two or more employers or two or more contracts of service are, by virtue of regulations made under section 26(5) of that Act, to be treated as one ;

(*c*) any question arising under Part V of this Act (including Schedule 4 to this Act) or regulations under it as to—

(i) whether a person is, or was, an employee or employer of another ;

E 2

(ii) whether an employer is entitled to make any deduction from his contributions payments in accordance with regulations under Part I of Schedule 4 ;

(iii) whether a payment falls to be made to an employer in accordance with the regulations ;

(iv) the amount that falls to be so deducted or paid ;

(v) whether two or more employers or two or more contracts of service are, by virtue of regulations made under section 50(2) above, to be treated as one,

and any question arising under regulations made by virtue of paragraph (c), (d) or (f) of section 46(8) above.

Section 66.

SCHEDULE 6

Christmas Bonus for Pensioners

Interpretation

1.—(1) In this Schedule " qualifying benefit " means—

1975 c. 14

(a) any of the following benefits under the Social Security Act 1975—

(i) a retirement pension ;

(ii) an invalidity pension ;

(iii) a widowed mother's allowance or widow's pension ;

(iv) a severe disablement allowance ;

(v) an invalid care allowance ;

(vi) an industrial death benefit by way of widow's or widower's pension ;

(b) an attendance allowance ;

(c) an unemployability supplement or allowance ;

(d) a war disablement pension ;

(e) a war widow's pension ;

(f) income support.

(2) In this Schedule—

" attendance allowance " means—

(a) an attendance allowance under section 35 of the Social Security Act 1975 ;

(b) an increase of disablement pension under section 61 or 63 of that Act (increases in respect of the need for constant attendance) ;

(c) a payment under regulations made in exercise of the power in section 159(3)(b) of that Act (constant attendance allowance and an increase for exceptionally severe disablement for certain pre-1948 cases) ;

(*d*) an increase of allowance under Article 8 of the   Sch 6
Pneumoconiosis, Byssinosis and Miscellaneous Diseases S.I. 1983/136.
Benefit Scheme 1983 (constant attendance allowance for
certain persons to whom that Scheme applies) or under the
corresponding provision of any Scheme which may replace
that Scheme ;

(*e*) an allowance in respect of constant attendance on
account of disablement for which a person is in receipt
of war disablement pension, including an allowance in
respect of exceptionally severe disablement ;

" married couple " and " unmarried couple " are to be construed in accordance with Part II of this Act and any
regulations made under it.

" pensionable age " means—

(*a*) in the case of a man, the age of 65 ;

(*b*) in the case of a woman, the age of 60 ;

" retirement pension " includes graduated retirement benefit, if
paid periodically ;

" unemployability supplement or allowance " means—

(*a*) an unemployability supplement payable under section 58 of
the Social Security Act 1975 by virtue of paragraph 4 of 1975 c. 14.
Schedule 3 to this Act ; or

(*b*) any corresponding allowance payable—

(i) by virtue of section 7(3)(*a*) of the Industrial Injuries 1975 c. 16.
and Diseases (Old Cases) Act 1975 ;

(ii) by way of supplement to retired pay or pension ex-
empt from income tax under section 365(1) of the Income 1970 c. 10.
and Corporation Taxes Act 1970 ;

(iii) under the Personal Injuries (Emergency Provisions) 1939 c. 82.
Act 1939 ; or

(iv) by way of supplement to retired pay or pension
under the Polish Resettlement Act 1947 ;   1947 c. 19.

and each of the following expressions, namely " attendance allowance ", " unemployability supplement or allowance ", " war disablement pension " and " war widow's pension ", includes any payment which the Secretary of State accepts as being analogous to it.

(3) In this Schedule " the relevant week ", in relation to any year,
means the week beginning with the first Monday in December or
such other week as may be specified in an order made by the Secretary of State.

Entitlement

2.—(1) Any person who in any year—

(*a*) is present or ordinarily resident in the United Kingdom or
any other member state at any time during the relevant
week ; and

(*b*) is entitled to a payment of a qualifying benefit in respect
of a period which includes a day in that week or is to be

treated as entitled to a payment of a qualifying benefit in respect of such a period,

shall, subject to the following provisions of this Schedule, be entitled to payment under this sub-paragraph in respect of that year.

(2) Subject to the following provisions of this Schedule, any person who is a member of a married or unmarried couple and is entitled to a payment under sub-paragraph (1) above in respect of a year shall also be entitled to payment under this sub-paragraph in respect of that year if—

> (*a*) both members of the couple have attained pensionable age not later than the end of the relevant week ; and

> (*b*) the other member of the couple satisfies the condition mentioned in sub-paragraph (1)(*a*) above ; and

> (*c*) either—

>> (i) he is entitled or treated as entitled, in respect of the other member of the couple to an increase in the payment of the qualifying benefit ; or

>> (ii) the only qualifying benefit to which he is entitled is income support.

(3) A payment under sub-paragraph (1) or (2) above—

> (*a*) is to be made by the Secretary of State ; and

> (*b*) is to be of £10 or such larger sum as the Secretary of State may by order specify.

(4) Where the only qualifying benefit to which a person is entitled is income support, he shall not be entitled to a payment under sub-paragraph (1) above unless he has attained pensionable age not later than the end of the relevant week.

(5) Only one sum shall be payable in respect of any person.

3.—(1) For the purposes of paragraph 2 above the Channel Islands, the Isle of Man and Gibraltar shall be treated as though they were part of the United Kingdom.

(2) A person shall be treated for the purposes of paragraph 2(1) (*b*) above as entitled to a payment of a qualifying benefit if he would be so entitled—

> (*a*) in the case of a qualifying benefit other than income support—

>> (i) but for the fact that he or, if he is a member of a married or unmarried couple, the other member is entitled to receive some other payment out of public funds ;

>> (ii) but for the operation of section 30(1) of the Social Security Act 1975 ;

>> (iii) but for the fact that he has not made a claim for the payment ;

> (*b*) in the case of income support, but for the fact that his income or, if he is a member of a married or unmarried couple, the income of the other member of the couple was

1975 c. 14.

exceptionally of an amount which resulted in his having
ceased to be entitled to income support.

(3) A person shall be treated for the purposes of paragraph
2(2)(*c*)(i) above as entitled in respect of the other member of the
couple to an increase in a payment of qualifying benefit if he would
be so entitled—

(*a*) but for the fact that he or the other member is entitled to
receive some other payment out of public funds ;

(*b*) but for the operation of any provision of section 30(1), 45(2)
or (2A) or 66(4) of the Social Security Act 1975 or any
regulations made under section 66(3) of that Act whereby
entitlement to benefit is affected by the amount of a person's
earnings in a given period ; or

(*c*) but for such terms as are mentioned in sub-paragraph (2)
(*a*)(iii) above ; or

(*d*) but for the fact that he has not made a claim for the increase.

(4) For the purposes of paragraph 2 above a person shall be
deemed not to be entitled to a payment of a war disablement pension
unless not later than the end of the relevant week—

(*a*) he has attained the age of 70 in the case of a man or 65 in
the case of a woman ; or

(*b*) he is treated under section 27(3) of the Social Security Act
1975 as having retired from regular employment.

(5) A sum payable under paragraph 2 above shall not be treated
as benefit for the purposes of any enactment or instrument under
which entitlement to the relevant qualifying benefit arises or is to
be treated as arising.

(6) A payment and the right to receive a payment—

(*a*) under paragraph 2 above or any enactment corresponding
to it in Northern Ireland ; or

(*b*) under regulations relating to widows which are made by
the Secretary of State under any enactment relating to police
and which contain a statement that the regulations provide
for payments corresponding to payments under that paragraph,

shall be disregarded for all purposes of income tax and for the
purposes of any enactment or instrument under which regard is had
to a person's means.

Administration of payments

4.—(1) A determination by the competent authority that a person
is entitled or not entitled to payment of a qualifying benefit in respect
of a period which includes a day in the relevant week shall be conclusive for the purposes of paragraph 2 above ; and in this sub-
paragraph " competent authority " means, in relation to a payment
of any description of qualifying benefit, an authority who ordinarily
determines whether a person is entitled to such a payment.

(2) Any question arising under this Schedule other than one determined or falling to be determined under sub-paragraph (1) above

shall be determined by the Secretary of State whose decision shall except as provided by the following sub-paragraph be final.

(3) The Secretary of State may reverse a decision under sub-paragraph (2) above on new facts being brought to his notice or if he is satisfied that the decision was given in ignorance of, or was based on a mistake as to, some material fact.

Section 73.

SCHEDULE 7

SUPPLEMENTARY BENEFIT ETC.

Interpretation

1. In this Schedule—

1946 c. 67.
1965 c. 57.

" the former National Insurance Acts " means the National Insurance Act 1946 and the National Insurance Act 1965 ; and

1946 c. 62.
1965 c. 52.

" the former Industrial Injuries Acts " means the National Insurance (Industrial Injuries) Act 1946 and the National Insurance (Industrial Injuries) Act 1965.

Prevention of duplication of payments

2. Section 27 above shall have effect in relation to supplementary benefit as it has effect in relation to income support.

Claims and Payments

3.—(1) Section 51 above shall have effect in relation to the benefits specified in sub-paragraph (2) below as it has effect· in relation to the benefits to which it applies by virtue of subsection (2).

(2) The benefits mentioned in sub-paragraph (1) above are benefits under—

    (*a*) the former National Insurance Acts ;

    (*b*) the former Industrial Injuries Acts ;

1948 c. 29.   (*c*) the National Assistance Act 1948 ;

1966 c. 20.   (*d*) the Supplementary Benefit Act 1966 ;

1976 c. 71.   (*e*) the Supplementary Benefits Act 1976 ;

1970 c. 55.   (*f*) the Family Income Supplements Act 1970.

Adjudication

4.—(1) Section 52(3) above shall have effect for the purposes of the benefits specified in paragraph 3(2) above as it has effect for the purposes of benefit under the Social Security Act 1975.

1975 c. 14.

(2) Procedure regulations made under section 115 of the Social Security Act 1975 by virtue of sub-paragraph (1) above may make different provision in relation to each of the benefits specified in paragraph 3(2) above.

Overpayments

5.—(1) Section 53 above shall have effect in relation to the benefits specified in paragraph 3(2) above as it has effect in relation to the benefits to which it applies by virtue of subsection (10).

(2) The reference to housing benefit in section 29(4) includes a   Sch. 7
reference to housing benefits under Part II of the Social Security 1982 c. 24.
and Housing Benefits Act 1982.

Legal proceedings

6. Section 56 above shall have effect as if the benefit Acts included—

    (a) the National Assistance Act 1948 ;   1948 c. 29.
    (b) the Supplementary Benefit Act 1966 ;   1966 c. 20.
    (c) the Supplementary Benefits Act 1976 ;   1976 c. 71.
    (d) the Family Income Supplements Act 1970.   1970 c. 55.

Inspection

7. Section 58 above shall have effect as if the benefit Acts included the Acts mentioned in paragraph 6(c) and (d) above.

Up-rating

8. Section 63 above shall have effect as if the sums mentioned in subsection (1) included sums payable by way of benefit under—

    (a) the Family Income Supplements Act 1970 ;
    (b) the Supplementary Benefits Act 1976 ; and
    (c) Part II of the Social Security and Housing Benefits Act 1982.

SCHEDULE 8   Section 75.

EARNINGS FACTORS

Social Security Act 1975 (c. 14)

1. The Social Security Act 1975 shall be amended as follows.

2.—(1) In subsection (2) of section 13 (contribution conditions and the earnings factor) for the words from "from" to "above" there shall be substituted the words " in respect of each tax year from those of his earnings upon which primary Class 1 contributions have been paid or treated as paid and from Class 2 and Class 3 contributions ".

(2) In subsection (3) of that section, for the words from " primary " to the end there shall be substituted the words " earnings upon which primary Class 1 contributions are paid at the reduced rate ".

(3) In subsection (4), for the words " contributions of any class " there shall be substituted the words " earnings or Class 2 or Class 3 contributions ".

(4) In subsection (5)—

    (a) for the word " contributions ", in the first place where it occurs, there shall be substituted the words " earnings or Class 2 or Class 3 contributions " ;
    (b) paragraph (a) shall be omitted ; and

(c) for the words from " shall be derived " to the end of the subsection there shall be substituted the words " may be derived—

> (i) from earnings upon which primary Class 1 contributions have been paid or treated as paid ;
>
> (ii) from earnings which have been credited ;
>
> (iii) from contributions of different classes paid or credited in the same tax year ;
>
> (iv) by any combination of the methods mentioned in sub-paragraphs (i) to (iii) above.".

(5) The following subsection shall be inserted after subsection (5A)—

> " (5B) Regulations may provide for requiring persons to maintain, in such form and manner as may be prescribed, records of such earnings paid by them as are relevant for the purpose of calculating earnings factors, and to retain such records for so long as may be prescribed.".

(6) In subsection (6)(c)—

(a) for the words " person's contribution of any class or classes " there shall be substituted the word " person " ;

(b) for the words " those contributions " there shall be substituted the words " his earnings upon which primary Class 1 contributions have been paid or treated as paid and from his Class 2 and Class 3 contributions ".

3.—(1) The following paragraph shall be substituted for sub-paragraph (2)(b) of paragraph 1 (unemployment and sickness benefit) of Schedule 3 (contribution conditions)—

> " (b) the earnings factor derived—
>
> > (i) in the case of unemployment benefit, from earnings upon which primary Class 1 contributions have been paid or treated as paid; and
> >
> > (ii) in the case of sickness benefit, from such earnings or from Class 2 contributions,
>
> must be not less than that year's lower earnings limit multiplied by 25.".

(2) In sub-paragraph (3)(a) of that paragraph, after the word " class " there shall be inserted the words " or been credited with earnings ".

(3) The following paragraph shall be substituted for sub-paragraph (3)(b)—

> " (b) the earnings factor derived—
>
> > (i) in the case of unemployment benefit, from earnings upon which primary Class 1 contributions have been paid or treated as paid or from earnings credited ; and
> >
> > (ii) in the case of sickness benefit, from such earnings or from Class 2 contributions,
>
> must be not less than that year's lower earnings limit multiplied by 50.".

(4) In sub-paragraph (1)(*b*) of paragraph 4 of that Schedule for the words " those contributions " there shall be substituted the words " earnings upon which primary Class 1 contributions have been paid or treated as paid and from Class 2 and Class 3 contributions ".

SCH. 8

(5) In sub-paragraph (2)(*b*) of paragraph 5 of that Schedule (widowed mother's allowance, widow's pension and retirement pensions) for the words " those contributions " there shall be substituted the words " earnings upon which such of those contributions as are primary Class 1 contributions were paid or treated as paid and any Class 2 or Class 3 contributions ".

(6) The following paragraph shall be substituted for sub-paragraph (3)(*b*) of that paragraph—

" (*b*) in the case of each of those years, the earnings factor derived from—

(i) any earnings upon which such of those contributions as are primary Class 1 contributions were paid or treated as paid or earnings credited ; and

(ii) any Class 2 or Class 3 contributions for the year,

must be not less than the qualifying earnings factor for the year.".

(7) In paragraph 8(3) (satisfaction of certain contribution conditions in early years of contribution) for the words " his contributions of a relevant class " there shall be substituted the words " the aggregate of his earnings upon which primary Class 1 contributions were paid or treated as paid and from Class 2 contributions ".

Social Security Pensions Act 1975 (c. 60)

4. The Social Security Pensions Act 1975 shall be amended as follows.

5. In subsection (4) of section 3 (married women and widows) for the words from " contributions " to " rate " there shall be substituted the words " earnings upon which primary Class 1 contributions are paid at a reduced rate by virtue of regulations under subsection (2) above or from Class 2 contributions paid at a reduced rate by virtue of such regulations ".

6. In subsection (1) of section 5 of that Act (voluntary contributions) after the word " from " there shall be inserted the words " earnings upon which Class 1 contributions have been paid or treated as paid or from Class 2 ".

7.—(1) In section 6 (rate of Category A retirement pension)—

(*a*) in subsection (5), for the words " contributions actually paid by him in respect of that year " there shall be substituted the words " earnings upon which primary Class 1 contributions were paid or treated as paid in respect of that year and earnings factors derived from Class 2 and Class 3 contributions actually paid in respect of it " ; and

(*b*) subsection (5A) shall be omitted.

SCH. 8

8.—(1) In subsection (2) of section 35 (earner's guaranteed minimum) for the words " contributions paid in respect of such earnings as are mentioned in subsection (1) above " there shall be substituted the words " earnings such as are mentioned in subsection (1) above upon which primary Class 1 contributions have been paid or treated as paid ".

9. Section 43(1A) and section 47(2A) shall not apply to any period after the end of the tax year 1986-87.

10. In subsection (3)(*b*) of section 45 (premium where guaranteed minimum pension excluded from full revaluation) for the word " contributions ", in the first place where it occurs, there shall be substituted the words " earnings upon which primary Class 1 contributions have been paid or treated as paid ".

Social Security (Miscellaneous Provisions) Act 1977 (c. 5)

11. In subsection (1)(*b*) of section 21 of the Social Security (Miscellaneous Provisions) Act 1977 (calculation of guaranteed minimum pensions preserved under approved arrangements) after the word " contributions ", in the first place where it occurs, there shall be inserted the words " or earnings ".

Section 82.

SCHEDULE 9

NORTHERN IRELAND

PART I

APPEAL ON QUESTION OF LAW FROM MEDICAL APPEAL TRIBUNAL TO COMMISSIONER

1975 c. 15.

1. After section 112 of the Social Security (Northern Ireland) Act 1975 there shall be inserted the following section—

"Appeal etc. on question of law to Commissioner.

112A.—(1) Subject to this section, an appeal lies to a Commissioner from any decision of a medical appeal tribunal on the ground that the decision is erroneous in point of law, at the instance of—

    (*a*) an adjudication officer; or

    (*b*) the claimant ; or

    (*c*) a trade union of which the claimant was a member at the time of the relevant accident or, in a case relating to severe disablement allowance, at the prescribed time ; or

    (*d*) the Department.

(2) Subsection (1) above, as it applies to a trade union, applies also to any other association which exists to promote the interests and welfare of its members.

(3) No appeal lies under subsection (1) above without the leave—

    (*a*) of the person who was the chairman of the medical appeal tribunal when the decision was given or, in a case prescribed by regulations, the leave of some other chairman of a medical appeal tribunal ; or

(b) subject to and in accordance with regulations, of a Commissioner,

and regulations may make provision as to the manner in which, and the time within which, appeals are to be brought and applications made for leave to appeal.

(4) Where a question of law arises in a case before a medical appeal tribunal, the tribunal may refer that question to a Commissioner for his decision.

(5) On any such appeal or reference, the question of law arising for the decision of the Commissioner and the facts on which it arises shall be submitted for his consideration in the prescribed manner ; and the medical appeal tribunal on being informed in the prescribed manner of his decision on the question of law shall give, confirm or revise their decision on the case accordingly.

(6) No appeal lies under subsection (1) from a decision of a medical appeal tribunal given before the date of the coming into operation of Part I of Schedule 9 to the Social Security Act 1986.".

PART II

TRANSFER OF FUNCTIONS RELATING TO COMMISSIONERS

2.—(1) In this Part—

" the Commissioners " means the Chief and other Social Security Commissioners for Northern Ireland ;

" the Department ", except in the expression " the Department of Finance and Personnel ", means the Department of Health and Social Services for Northern Ireland.

(2) The references in paragraphs 3(1)(b) and 4 to service by any person as a Commissioner include references to service treated as service as a Commissioner under paragraph 5(2) of Schedule 10 to the Social Security (Northern Ireland) Act 1975 (service under former enactments). 1975 c. 15.

3.—(1) The following functions of the Department are hereby transferred to the Lord Chancellor—

(a) the functions of the Department under paragraphs 4, 6 and 7 of Schedule 10 to the Social Security (Northern Ireland) Act 1975 (payment of remuneration, expenses, and pensions of the Commissioners) ;

(b) the functions of the Department under the provisions of the Judicial Pensions Act (Northern Ireland) 1951 (lump sums and widow's and children's pensions) and paragraph 3 of Schedule 3 to the Administration of Justice Act 1973 (in- 1951 c. 20 (N.I.). 1973 c. 15.

crease of certain widow's and children's pensions) so far as
those provisions apply to service by any person as a
Commissioner ;

(c) the administration of the offices of the Commissioners, including the functions of the Department under paragraph 3
of Schedule 10 to the Social Security (Northern Ireland)
Act 1975 (payments in connection with work of tribunals
etc.) relating to the work of the Commissioners ;

(d) the making, under or for the purposes of the enactments
mentioned in sub-paragraph (2) below, of regulations with
respect to proceedings before the Commissioners, whether
for the determination of any matter or for leave to appeal
to or from the Commissioners.

(2) The enactments referred to in sub-paragraph (1)(d) above are—

(a) sections 6(1) and 10 of the Family Income Supplements Act
(Northern Ireland) 1971 ;

(b) section 5 of the National Insurance Measure (Northern
Ireland) 1974 ;

(c) sections 106(2), 112A and 115(1) of the Social Security
(Northern Ireland) Act 1975 ;

(d) Articles 9(1) and 24 of the Child Benefit (Northern Ireland)
Order 1975 ;

(e) the definition of " regulations " in Article 2(2), and Articles
4(1) and 19(1), of the Supplementary Benefits (Northern
Ireland) Order 1977 ;

(f) section 14 of the Social Security Act 1980 ;

(g) Article 11(1) of the Social Security (Northern Ireland) Order
1980 ;

(h) Article 6 of the Forfeiture (Northern Ireland) Order 1982 ;

(j) Articles 17(5) and 36 of the Social Security (Northern
Ireland) Order 1982 ;

4.—(1) The functions of the Department of Finance and Personnel,
so far as they relate to the functions transferred by paragraph 3 above,
are hereby transferred to the Treasury.

(2) The functions of the Department of Finance and Personnel
under the Judicial Pensions Act (Northern Ireland) 1951, so far as
it applies to service by any person as a Commissioner, are hereby
transferred to the Treasury.

5. The functions of the Secretary of State under paragraph 7(5) of
Schedule 10 to the Social Security (Northern Ireland) Act 1975 (power
of Secretary of State to require person retired on medical grounds to
resume duties of Commissioner) are hereby transferred to the Lord
Chancellor.

6.—(1) Subject to any Order made after the passing of this Act
by virtue of subsection (1)(a) of section 3 of the Northern Ireland

1975 c. 15.

1971 c. 8 (N.I.).

1974 c. 4 (N.I.).

S.I. 1975/1504
(N.I. 16).

S.I. 1977/2156
(N.I. 27).

1980 c. 30.

S.I. 1980/870
(N.I. 8).

S.I. 1982/1082
(N.I. 14).
S.I. 1982/1084
(N.I. 16).

1951 c. 20 (N.I.).

1973 c. 36.

Constitution Act 1973, the matters to which this paragraph applies shall not be transferred matters for the purposes of that Act but shall for the purposes of subsection (2) of that section be treated as specified in Schedule 3 to that Act.

(2) This paragraph applies to all matters relating to the Commissioners, including procedure and appeals, other than those specified in paragraph 9 of Schedule 2 to the Northern Ireland Constitution Act 1973.

7. Regulations made by the Lord Chancellor by virtue of this Part of this Schedule shall be subject to annulment in pursuance of a resolution of either House of Parliament in like manner as a statutory instrument and section 5 of the Statutory Instruments Act 1946 shall apply accordingly.

8.—(1) Enactments and instruments passed or made before the coming into operation of this Part of this Schedule shall have effect, so far as may be necessary for the purpose or in consequence of the transfers effected by this Part as if—

    (*a*) references to the Department or to the Secretary of State were references to the Lord Chancellor ; and

    (*b*) references to the Department of Finance and Personnel were references to the Treasury ; and

    (*c*) references to moneys appropriated by Measure of the Northern Ireland Assembly were references to money provided by Parliament and references to the Consolidated Fund of Northern Ireland were references to the Consolidated Fund of the United Kingdom.

(2) This Part of this Schedule shall not affect the validity of anything done (or having effect as done) by or in relation to the Department, the Department of Finance and Personnel or the Secretary of State before the coming into operation of this Part, and anything which at the time of the coming into operation of this Part is in process of being done by or in relation to either of those Departments or the Secretary of State may, if it relates to a function transferred by this Part, be continued by or in relation to the Lord Chancellor or the Treasury, as the case may require.

(3) Anything done (or having effect as done) by the Department, the Department of Finance and Personnel or the Secretary of State for the purpose of a function transferred by this Part of this Schedule, if in force at the coming into operation of this Part, shall have effect, as far as required for continuing its effect after the coming into operation of this Part, as if done by the Lord Chancellor or by the Treasury, as the case may require.

(4) The amendments specified in Part III of this Schedule are without prejudice to the generality of this paragraph.

PART III

CONSEQUENTIAL AMENDMENTS

Judicial Pensions Act (Northern Ireland) 1951 (c. 20) (N.I.)

9. In section 16 of the Judicial Pensions Act (Northern Ireland)

1951 (recommendation required for payments conditional on eligibility for Commissioners' pensions) for the words " Department of Health and Social Services " there shall be substituted the words " Lord Chancellor ".

Social Security (Northern Ireland) Act 1975 (c. 15)

10.—(1) In paragraphs 4, 6 and 7 of Schedule 10 to the Social Security (Northern Ireland) Act 1975 (payment of remuneration, expenses and pensions of the Commissioners)—

(a) for the word " Department " in each place where it occurs (except in the expression " Department of Finance ") there shall be substituted the words " Lord Chancellor " ;

(b) for the words " Department of Finance " in each place where they occur there shall be substituted the word " Treasury ".

(2) In sub-paragraph (1) of the said paragraph 6 for the words " moneys appropriated by Measure of the Northern Ireland Assembly " there shall be substituted the words " money provided by Parliament ".

(3) In sub-paragraph (5) of the said paragraph 7 for the words " Secretary of State " there shall be substituted the words " Lord Chancellor ".

Social Security Act 1980 (c. 30)

11. In section 14 of the Social Security Act 1980 (appeal from Commissioners etc. on point of law)—

(a) subsection (6) (which provides for modifying the preceding provisions of that section in relation to decisions of medical appeal tribunals appointed under the Social Security (Northern Ireland) Act 1975) shall cease to have effect ;

1975 c. 15.

(b) in subsection (7) (which provides for modifying subsections (3) and (5) of that section in relation to decisions of Commissioners on questions of law referred by medical appeal tribunals) after the words " to a Commissioner)" there shall be inserted the words " and in relation to a decision of a Commissioner within the meaning of the Social Security (Northern Ireland) Act 1975 which was given in consequence of a reference under subsection (4) of section 112A of that Act (which makes corresponding provision for Northern Ireland)" ;

(c) in subsection (8) (which provides for the making of regulations)—

(i) in paragraph (b), for the words from " or a medical appeal tribunal " to " for Northern Ireland " there shall be substituted the words " by the Lord Chancellor " ;

(ii) the words from " negative resolution " to the end there shall be substituted the words " annulment in pursuance of a resolution of either House of Parliament in like manner as a statutory instrument and section 5 of the

1946 c. 36. Statutory Instruments Act 1946 shall apply accordingly.".

12. In paragraph 21 of Schedule 3 to that Act (regulations in SCH. 9
Northern Ireland corresponding to regulations in Great Britain
made by the Secretary of State not requiring prior submission to
Social Security Advisory Committee), after the words " Secretary
of State " there shall be inserted the words " or the Lord Chancellor ".

Forfeiture (Northern Ireland) Order 1982 (S.I. 1982/1082 (N.I. 14))

13. In Article 6(2) of the Forfeiture (Northern Ireland) Order 1982
(regulations for purposes of determinations by Social Security
Commissioner), for the words " Department of Health and Social
Services " there shall be substituted the words " Lord Chancellor ".

SCHEDULE 10   Section 86.

MINOR AND CONSEQUENTIAL AMENDMENTS

PART I

PENSIONS

Social Security Act 1973 (c. 38)

1. The Social Security Act 1973 shall be amended as follows.

2. In section 58(2) (linked qualifying service)—

   (a) the following paragraph shall be substituted for paragraph
      (a)—

      " (a) under the rules of a scheme applying to him in the
     earlier period of service—

        (i) there was made a transfer of his accrued rights
          under that scheme to another scheme applying
          to him in the later period of service ; or

        (ii) those rights were secured by a policy of insur-
          ance or an annuity contract and were sub-
          sequently transferred to another scheme apply-
          ing to him in the later period of service ; " ;
          and

   (b) in paragraph (b), for the words " that transfer " there shall
     be substituted the words " the transfer of his accrued rights
     to the second scheme.".

3. In section 64 (modification of occupational pension scheme by
order of Occupational Pensions Board) the following subsection shall
be inserted after subsection (1)—

   " (1A) The Board shall also have power on such an application
to make an order—

     (a) authorising the modification of the scheme with a view
       to achieving any one or more of such other purposes
       as may be prescribed ; or

     (b) modifying the scheme with a view to achieving any one
       or more of those purposes.".

F

4. In section 66—

(*a*) in subsection (1)(*a*), for the words " and the Pensions Act "
there shall be substituted the words ", the Pensions Act
and Part I of the Social Security Act 1986 " ;

(*b*) in subsection (7)(*a*), after the words " contracting-out certificates " there shall be inserted the words " and appropriate
scheme certificates " ; and

(*c*) the following subsection shall be substituted for subsection
(10)—

" (10) References in this section—

(*a*) to this Part of this Act, the Pensions Act and
Part I of the Social Security Act 1986 include
references to any provisions in force in Northern Ireland and corresponding to provisions of
this Part of this Act, the Pensions Act or Part
I of the Social Security Act 1986 ; and

(*b*) to contracting-out certificates and appropriate
scheme certificates include references to contracting-out certificates and appropriate scheme
certificates within the meaning of any such provisions.".

5. In section 67(1)(*a*) (review of determinations by Board) after the
words " contracting-out certificate " there shall be inserted the
words " or an appropriate scheme certificate ".

6. In section 69 (rule against perpetuities)—

(*a*) in subsection (1), for the words " an occupational " there
shall be substituted the words " a personal or occupational " ;

(*b*) in subsection (2), for the words " under this Part of this
Act " there shall be substituted the words " or an appropriate scheme under Part I of the Social Security Act
1986 " ; and

(*c*) in subsection (5), for the words " which ceases to be contracted-out, or " there shall be substituted the words " which
ceases—

(*a*) if it is an occupational pension scheme, to be contracted-out ; or

(*b*) if it is a personal pension scheme, to be an appropriate scheme,

or ".

7. Sections 70 (legal restrictions of doubtful application), 71
(friendly societies) and 72 (fees for official services to schemes)
shall have effect in relation to personal pension schemes as they
have effect in relation to occupational pension schemes.

8. In section 99(1) the following definitions shall be inserted at
the appropriate places—

" " appropriate scheme " shall be construed in accordance with
Part I of the Social Security Act 1986 ; " ; and

" " personal pension scheme " has the same meaning as in the
Social Security Act 1986 ; ".

9. In paragraph 4 of Schedule 16 (preservation of benefits under
occupational pension schemes)—

(*a*) for the words " requisite benefits " in the first place where
they occur in sub-paragraph (2) and in sub-paragraph (3)
there shall be substituted the words " a guaranteed minimum pension " ; and

(*b*) for the words " his requisite benefits " in sub-paragraph (2)
there shall be substituted the words " the guaranteed minimum pension ".

Social Security Act 1975 (c. 14)

10. In paragraph 6(1)(*h*) of Schedule 1 to the Social Security Act
1975 (regulations about return of contributions) after the word " of ",
in the first place where it occurs, there shall be inserted the words
" the whole or any prescribed part of any ".

Social Security Pensions Act 1975 (c. 60)

11. The Social Security Pensions Act 1975 shall be amended as
follows.

12. In section 26 (contracting-out)—

(*a*) in subsection (1), for the words " the requisite benefits " there
shall be substituted the words " a guaranteed minimum
pension " ; and

(*b*) in subsection (2), for the words from the beginning to " such
pension " there shall be substituted the words " " Guaranteed minimum pension " means any pension which is provided by an occupational pension scheme in accordance
with the requirements of sections 33 and 36 below ".

13. In section 27(4) (contracted-out rates of Class 1 contributions)
for the words from the beginning to " that employment " there shall
be substituted the words " Where—

(*a*) an earner has ceased to be employed in an employment ;
and

(*b*) earnings are paid to him or for his benefit within the period
of 6 weeks, or such other period as may be prescribed, from
the day on which he so ceased,

that employment ".

14. In section 29 (contracted-out rates of benefit)—

(*a*) in subsection (1)(*a*), for the words " or a widow's pension "
there shall be substituted the words ", a widow's pension
or a widower's invalidity pension under section 16 above " ;

(*b*) in subsection (2)—

(i) after the words " this section " there shall be inserted the words " and sections 16(2B), 28(7A) and
59(1A) of the principal Act " ; and

(ii) at the end there shall be added the words " or if as
a result of a transfer payment or transfer under regulations made by virtue of section 38 below he is no longer

F 2

entitled to guaranteed minimum pensions under the scheme by which the transfer payment or transfer is made and has not as a result of the transfer payment or transfer become entitled to guaranteed minimum pensions under the scheme to which the transfer payment or transfer is made."

15. In section 30(1)(*a*) (contracted-out employment) for the words " the requisite benefits of " there shall be substituted the words " a guaranteed minimum pension provided by ".

16. In section 32 (contracted-out schemes)—

(*a*) in subsection (2)—

(i) for the words " the requisite benefits " in paragraph (*a*) ; and

(ii) for the words " requisite benefits " in paragraph (*b*), there shall be substituted the words " guaranteed minimum pensions " ;

(*b*) in subsection (4) the words " relating to the scheme or its management " shall cease to have effect.

17. In section 33 (requirements for contracting-out) the following subsection shall be inserted after subsection (1)—

" (1A) In the case of an earner who is a married woman or widow who is liable to pay primary Class 1 contributions at a reduced rate by virtue of section 3 of this Act, subject to the provisions of this Part of this Act, for a scheme to be contracted-out in relation to her employment it must—

(*a*) provide for her to be entitled to a pension under the scheme if she attains pensionable age ; and

(*b*) satisfy such other conditions as may be prescribed.".

18. The following subsection shall be substituted for section 38(1) (transfer of accrued rights)—

" (1) Regulations may prescribe circumstances in which and conditions subject to which—

(*a*) there may be made by one occupational pension scheme to another or by an occupational pension scheme to a personal pension scheme a transfer of or a transfer payment in respect of—

(i) an earner's accrued rights to guaranteed minimum pensions under a contracted-out scheme ;

(ii) an earner's accrued rights to pensions under an occupational pension scheme which is not contracted-out, to the extent that those rights derive from his accrued rights to guaranteed minimum pensions under a contracted-out scheme ; or

(iii) the liability for the payment of guaranteed minimum pensions to or in respect of any person who has become entitled to them ;

(*b*) there may be made to an occupational pension scheme or a personal pension scheme a transfer of or a trans-

fer payment in respect of an earner's accrued rights to
guaranteed minimum pensions which are appropriately
secured for the purposes of section 52C below.".

19. Sections 41(4) and 49(3) and (7) (powers of Occupational
Pensions Board which are no longer required) shall cease to have
effect.

20. In section 41A(4) of that Act (protection of earner's pensions)
" 2 " shall be substituted for " 5 ".

21. In section 42(1)(*b*) (premium on termination of contracted-out
employment) for the word " five " there shall be substituted the
word " two ".

22. In section 43(2A) (linked qualifying service)—

   (*a*) the following paragraph shall be substituted for paragraph
      (*a*)—
         " (*a*) under the rules of a scheme applying to him in
      the earlier period of service—
         (i) there was made a transfer of his accrued rights
            under that scheme to another scheme applying to
            him in the later period of service ; or
         (ii) those rights were secured by a policy of insur-
            ance or an annuity contract and were subse-
            quently transferred to another scheme applying
            to him in the later period of service ; " ; and

   (*b*) in paragraph (*b*), for the words " that transfer " there shall
      be substituted the words " transfer of his accrued rights to
      the second scheme ".

23.—(1) In subsection (1) of section 44 (premium on termination
of contracted-out scheme) after the word " is " there shall be inserted
the words " or has been " and after the words " for the event of "
there shall be inserted the words ", or in connection with,".

(2) The following subsections shall be inserted after subsection (1B)
of that section (arrangements for scheme's ceasing to be contracted-
out)—

   " (1C) If the scheme ceases to be a contracted-out scheme
   (whether by being wound up or otherwise) and the Occupational
   Pensions Board either—

      (*a*) have withdrawn their approval of previously approved
         arrangements relating to it ; or

      (*b*) have declined to approve arrangements relating to it,

   the Board may issue a certificate to that effect.

   (1D) A certificate issued under subsection (1C)(*a*) or (*b*) above
   shall be cancelled by the Board if they subsequently approve
   the arrangements.".

(3) In subsection (2)(*a*) of that section, after the word " under ",
in the second place where it occurs, there shall be inserted the words
" section 52C of or ".

(4) In subsection (5) of that section, for the words "The amount" there shall be substituted the words "Subject to subsection (5A) below, the amount".

(5) The following subsections shall be inserted after that subsection—

"(5A) Where in calculating the costs referred to in subsection (5) above the Secretary of State cannot readily ascertain the amount of any earnings in a tax week, he may make the calculation as if the amount of those earnings were equal to the upper earnings limit for that tax week, and may certify the costs accordingly.

(5B) Where—

   (*a*) the Secretary of State subsequently ascertains the amount of those earnings ; and

   (*b*) it appears to him that the amount of the premium would have been less if he had not made the calculation on the basis described in subsection (5A) above,

he shall refund to the prescribed person the amount by which it would have been less.".

24. The following subsection shall be inserted after section 49(2) of that Act (duty to supervise schemes which have ceased to be contracted-out)—

"(2A) Where in the case of any scheme the Board have issued a certificate under subsection (1C) of section 44 above which has not been cancelled under subsection (1D) of that section, or a certificate under subsection (2) of section 44ZA above which has not been cancelled under subsection (3) of that section, the Board shall not be under the duty which would otherwise be imposed on them by subsection (2) above in relation to that scheme.".

25. In section 50 (alteration of rules of contracted-out schemes)—

   (*a*) in subsection (1)—

      (i) after the word "Board" there shall be inserted the words "unless it is an alteration to which this subsection does not apply" ; and

      (ii) for the words "such alteration" there shall be substituted the words "alteration to which this subsection applies" ; and

   (*b*) the following subsection shall be inserted after that subsection—

      "(1A) Subsection (1) above does not apply—

1984 c. 48.
1985 c. 53.

      (*a*) to an alteration consequential on a provision of the Health and Social Security Act 1984, the Social Security Act 1985 or the Social Security Act 1986 ; or

      (*b*) to an alteration of a prescribed description.".

26.—(1) Section 52C (cases where scheme's liability is discharged) shall have effect and shall be deemed always to have had effect as if the following subsections were substituted for subsections (1) to (3)—

> "(1) A transaction to which this section applies discharges the trustees or managers of an occupational pension scheme from their liability to provide for or in respect of any person either the requisite benefits or short service benefit or any alternative to short service benefit—
>
> > (*a*) if it is carried out not earlier than the time when that person's pensionable service terminates ; and
> >
> > (*b*) if and to the extent that it results in—
> >
> > > (i) the requisite benefits ; or
> > >
> > > (ii) short service benefit, or an alternative to short service benefit, for or in respect of that person being appropriately secured ; and
> >
> > (*c*) in a case where the transaction takes place on or after 1st January 1986, if and to the extent that the requirements set out in any one of paragraphs (*a*), (*b*) and (*c*) of subsection (5) below are satisfied.
>
> (2) This section applies to the following transactions—
>
> > (*a*) the taking out or the transfer of the benefit of a policy of insurance or a number of such policies ;
> >
> > (*b*) the entry into or the transfer of the benefit of an annuity contract or a number of such contracts.".

(2) Subsection (5) of that section shall have effect and shall be deemed always to have had effect as if "(1)" were substituted for "(2)(*b*)".

(3) In relation to transactions which take place after the commencement of section 8 above section 52C(1) of the Social Security Pensions Act 1975 shall have effect with the substitution of the words "guaranteed minimum pensions" for the words "the requisite benefits", in both places where they occur.

27.—(1) Subsection (1) of section 52D (supplementary provisions) shall have effect and shall be deemed always to have had effect—

> (*a*) as if the following paragraph were substituted for paragraph (*b*)—
>
> > "(*b*) either—
> >
> > > (i) the transaction wholly or partly securing them was carried out before 1st January 1986 and discharged the trustees or managers of the scheme as mentioned in subsection (1) of that section ; or
> > >
> > > (ii) it is carried out on or after that date without any of the requirements specified in subsection (5)(*a*) to (*c*) of that section being satisfied in relation to it and the scheme has been wound up ; " ; and
>
> (*b*) as if for the words from "entitled" to "which" there were substituted the words "only entitled to such part (if any) of his or her guaranteed minimum pension as".

(2) In that subsection after the words " purposes of " there shall be inserted the words " sections 16(2B), 28(7A) and 59(1A) of the principal Act and ".

28. The following definition shall be inserted after the definition of " occupational pension scheme " in section 66(1)—

" " personal pension scheme " has the meaning assigned to it by section 84(1) of the Social Security Act 1986 ; ".

29. At the end of paragraph 5(1) of Part I of Schedule 1A (revalution of pensions) there shall be added the words " and which is not an average salary benefit ".

30. In Part II of Schedule 1A (transfer values)—

(*a*) the following sub-paragraphs shall be inserted after paragraph 12(2)—

" (2A) Where a member continues in employment to which a scheme applies after his pensionable service in that employment terminates—

(*a*) if regulations so provide, he only acquires a right to the cash equivalent of such part of the benefits specified in sub-paragraph (1) above as may be prescribed ; and

(*b*) if regulations so provide, he acquires no right to a cash equivalent.

(2B) Regulations may provide for the purposes of sub-paragraph (2A) above that in prescribed circumstances a number of employments (whether or not consecutive) shall be treated as a single employment." ;

(*b*) paragraph 12(4) and the reference to it in paragraph 12(3) shall be omitted and shall be deemed never to have been included ;

(*c*) in paragraph 13—

(i) in paragraph (*c*) of sub-paragraph (2), for the words " such other type or types of pension arrangements as may be prescribed " there shall be substituted the words " other pension arrangements which satisfy prescribed requirements " ; and

(ii) the following sub-paragraph shall be inserted after that sub-paragraph—

" (2A) Without prejudice to the generality of sub-paragraph (2) above, the powers conferred by that sub-paragraph include power to provide that a scheme, an annuity or pension arrangements must satisfy requirements of the Inland Revenue." ;

(iii) in sub-paragraph (5)(*b*), for the word " them " there shall be substituted the words " the trustees or managers of the scheme from which he is being transferred " ; and

(*d*) in paragraph 14—

(i) in sub-paragraph (1), for the words " The cash

equivalents mentioned in paragraph 12(1) above " there shall be substituted the words " Cash equivalents " ;

(ii) at the end of sub-paragraph (2), there shall be added (but not as part of paragraph (c)) the words " and power to provide that they shall be calculated and verified in accordance with guidance prepared by a prescribed body," ; and

(iii) the following paragraph shall be substituted for sub-paragraph (3)(*b*)—

" (*b*) that in prescribed circumstances a cash equivalent shall be increased or reduced.".

Employment Protection (Consolidation) Act 1978 (c. 44)

31.—(1) In the following provisions of the Employment Protection (Consolidation) Act 1978 (which all relate to payments to pension schemes of contributions which are unpaid on employer's insolvency) the words " or a personal pension scheme " shall be inserted after the words " an occupational pension scheme "—

(*a*) section 123(1) and (3) ;

(*b*) section 124(2) ;

(*c*) section 125(3) ; and

(*d*) section 126(1).

(2) In section 123(2) of that Act for the words " in accordance with an occupational pension scheme " there shall be substituted the words " to an occupational pension scheme or a personal pension scheme ".

(3) In section 127(3) of that Act the following definition shall be inserted after the definition of " occupational pension scheme "—

" " personal pension scheme " means any scheme or arrangement which is comprised in one or more instruments or agreements and which has, or is capable of having, effect so as to provide benefits, in the form of pensions or otherwise, payable on death or retirement to or in respect of employees who have made arrangements with the trustees or managers of the scheme for them to become members of the scheme ; ".

PART II

INCOME-RELATED BENEFITS

National Assistance Act 1948 (c.29)

32.—(1) In subsection (3) of section 22 of the National Assistance Act 1948 (charges to be made for local authority accommodation) for the words "(apart from any supplementation of his resources which he will receive under the Supplementary Benefits Act 1976" there shall be substituted the words "(disregarding income support)". 1976 c. 71.

(2) At the end of subsection (5) of that section there shall be added the words " except that, until the first such regulations come into force, a local authority shall give effect to Part III of Schedule 1

to the Supplementary Benefits Act 1976, as it had effect immediately before the amendments made by Schedule 2 to the Social Security Act 1980.

33. The words ",whether before or after the commencement of the Supplementary Benefits Act 1976," shall be omitted from subsection (6) of section 43 of that Act (recovery of cost of assistance from persons liable for maintenance).

Maintenance Orders Act 1950 (c.37)

34. In subsection (1) of section 3 of the Maintenance Orders Act 1950 (jurisdiction of English courts to make affiliation orders) after " 1976" there shall be inserted the words " or section 25 of the Social Security Act 1986 ".

35. In section 4 of that Act (jurisdiction of English courts to make affiliation orders against persons in Scotland or Northern Ireland)—

(a) the following paragraph shall be added at the end of subsection (1)—

" (d) for an order under section 24 of the Social Security Act 1986 (which provides for the recovery of expenditure on income support from such persons);" and

(b) in subsection (2), after the words " or the said section 18 " there shall be inserted the words " or the said section 24 ".

36. In section 9 of that Act—

(a) the following paragraph shall be added at the end of subsection (1)—

" (d) for an order under section 24 of the Social Security Act 1986 (which provides for the recovery of expenditure on income support from such persons);" and

(b) in subsection (2), after the words " or the said section 18 " there shall be inserted the words " or the said section 24 ".

37. In section 11(1) of that Act (jurisdiction of Northern Ireland courts to make affiliation orders) after "1977" there shall be inserted the words "or any enactment applying in Northern Ireland and corresponding to section 25 of the Social Security Act 1986".

38. In section 12 of that Act (jurisdiction of Northern Ireland courts to make affiliation orders against persons in England or Scotland)—

(a) the following paragraph shall be added at the end of subsection (1)—

"(d) for an order under any enactment applying in Northern Ireland and corresponding to section 24 of the Social Security Act 1986 (which provides for the recovery of expenditure on income support from such persons) ; " and

(b) the words " or of any order falling within subsection (1)
(d) of this section " shall be added at the end of subsection (2).

39. In section 16(2) of that Act (enforcement of maintenance orders)—

   (*a*) the following sub-paragraph shall be inserted after paragraph (*a*)(vii)—

   " (viii) section 24 of the Social Security Act 1986 or section 4 of the Affiliation Proceedings Act 1957 on an application made under section 25(1) of the Act of 1986 ; " ;

   (*b*) the following sub-paragraph shall be inserted after paragraph (*b*)(viii)—

   " (ix) an order made on an application under section 24 of the Social Security Act 1986 ; " ; and

   (*c*) the following sub-paragraph shall be inserted after paragraph (*c*)(vii)—

   "(viii) any enactment applying in Northern Ireland and corresponding to section 24 of the Social Security Act 1986 ; ".

Ecclesiastical Jurisdiction Measure 1963 (No. 1)

40. In subsection (7) of section 55 of the Ecclesiastical Jurisdiction Measure 1963, as amended by section 1 of the Ecclesiastical Jurisdiction (Amendment) Measure 1974, (deprivation etc. of priests etc. after certain proceedings) in the definition of "affiliation order" the word "or" shall be omitted and at the end there shall be inserted the words " or section 25 of the Social Security Act 1986 ".

Social Work (Scotland) Act 1968 (c.49)

41.—(1) In section 78(2A) of the Social Work (Scotland) Act 1968 (duty to make contributions in respect of children in care etc.) for words from " of " where second occurring to the end there shall be substituted the words " of income support or family credit.".

(2) In section 87(3) of that Act (charges for service and accommodation)—

   (*a*) after the word " by " where first occurring there shall be inserted the words " the Schedule to the Housing (Homeless Persons) Act 1977, paragraph 2(1) of Schedule 4 to the Social Security Act 1980, " ;

   (*b*) after " 1983 " there shall be inserted " and paragraph 32 of Schedule 10 to the Social Security Act 1986 " ; and

   (*c*) for the words " to 44 " there shall be substituted the words " (as amended by paragraph 5 of Schedule 1 to the Law Reform (Parent and Child) (Scotland) Act 1986) and 43 ".

Administration of Justice Act 1970 (c. 31)

42. In Schedule 8 to the Administration of Justice Act 1970 (maintenance orders)—

    (*a*) in paragraph 5, the word "or" shall be omitted from both places where it occurs and after "1975" there shall be inserted the words " or section 25 of the Social Security Act 1986 " ; and

    (*b*) in paragraph 6, the word "or", where first occurring, shall be omitted and after " 1976 " there shall be inserted the words " or section 24 of the Social Security Act 1986 ".

Attachment of Earnings Act 1971 (c. 32)

43. In Schedule 1 to the Attachment of Earnings Act 1971 (maintenance orders)—

    (*a*) in paragraph 6, the word " or " shall be omitted from both places where it occurs and after "1976" there shall be inserted the words " or section 25 of the Social Security Act 1986 " ; and

    (*b*) in paragraph 7, the word "or" where first occurring shall be omitted and after " 1976 " there shall be inserted the words " or section 24 of the Social Security Act 1986 ".

Housing (Financial Provisions) (Scotland) Act 1972 (c. 46)

44.—(1) In section 24(1)(*a*) of the Housing (Financial Provisions) (Scotland) Act 1972 (amount to be carried to credit of rent rebate account) for the words " under section 32 of the Social Security and Housing Benefits Act 1982 " there shall be substituted the words " under section 30 of the Social Security Act 1986 ".

(2) In section 25(1)(*a*) of that Act (amount to be carried to credit of rent allowance account) for the words " under section 32 of the Social Security and Housing Benefits Act 1982 " there shall be substituted the words " under section 30 of the Social Security Act 1986 ".

Employment and Training Act 1973 (c. 50)

45. In section 12(2)(*b*) of the Employment and Training Act 1973 (ancillary and transitional provisions) for the words " supplementary benefit within the meaning of the Supplementary Benefits Act 1976 " there shall be substituted the words " income support ".

Legal Aid Act 1974 (c. 4)

46. In each of the following provisions of the Legal Aid Act 1974, for the words from " supplementary " to " 1970 " there shall be substituted the words " income support or family credit "—

    (*a*) section 1(1)(*b*) ;

    (*b*) section 4(2) ;

    (*c*) section 11(5).

47. In paragraph 3(*c*) of Part I of Schedule 1 to that Act for the words " 18 of the Supplementary Benefits Act 1976 " there shall be substituted the words " 24 of the Social Security Act 1986 ".

Social Security Act 1975 (c. 14)

48. The following provisions of the Social Security Act 1975—

(*a*) section 87 (benefits to be inalienable) ; and

(*b*) section 165A(1) (necessity of claim for entitlement),

shall have effect in relation to income-related benefits as they have effect in relation to benefits under that Act.

Local Government (Scotland) Act 1975 (c. 30)
Rating (Disabled Persons) Act 1978 (c. 40)

49. The words " the housing benefit scheme (whether or not modified under section 28 of the Social Security Act 1986) " shall be substituted for the words " a scheme made under section 28(1)(*a*) of the Social Security and Housing Benefits Act 1982 (whether or not modified under section 30(1)(*a*) of that Act) "—

(*a*) in section 8(4) of the Local Government (Scotland) Act 1975 (payment of rates by instalments) ;

(*b*) in section 1(6) of the Rating (Disabled Persons) Act 1978 (rebates for hereditaments with special facilities for disabled persons) ; and

(*c*) in section 4(9) of that Act (rebates for lands and heritages with special facilities for disabled persons).

Employment Protection (Consolidation) Act 1978 (c.44)

50. In section 132 of the Employment Protection (Consolidation) Act 1978 (recoupment of benefit)—

(*a*) in subsection (2)(*a*) and (*c*), for the words " supplementary benefit " there shall be substituted the words " income support " ;

(*b*) in subsection (3)—

(i) in paragraphs (*a*) and (*f*), for the words " supplementary benefit " there shall be substituted the words " income support " ; and

(ii) in paragraph (*e*), for the words from " who " to the end of the paragraph there shall be substituted the words " a right of appeal to a social security appeal tribunal against any decision of an adjudication officer as to the total or partial recoupment of income support in pursuance of the regulations ; " ; and

(*c*) in subsection (4), for the words from " supplementary benefit ", in the first place where those words occur, to the end there shall be substituted the words " income support, no sum shall be recoverable under the Social Security Act 1986, and no abatement, payment or reduction shall be made by reference to the income support recouped.".

Child Care Act 1980 (c. 5)

51. The following subsection shall be substituted for subsection (1A) of section 45 of the Child Care Act 1980 (liability for contributions in respect of children in care)—

"(1A) A person shall not be liable under subsection (1) (i) above to make any contribution during any period when he is in receipt of income support or family credit.".

Local Government, Planning and Land Act 1980 (c. 65)

52.—(1) In section 54 of the Local Government, Planning and Land Act 1980 (rate support grant) in subsections (1) and (2) for the words "and subsidies under section 32(1)(*a*) of the Social Security and Housing Benefits Act 1982" there shall be substituted the words "and rate rebate subsidy under the Social Security Act 1986".

(2) The following paragraph shall be substituted for subsection (5)(*d*) of that section—

(*d*) subsection (10) or section 30 of the Social Security Act 1986 (power to exclude rate fund contributions under subsection (6) of that section and certain other items); ".

53. In section 154 of that Act (grant of rent rebates by urban developments corporations) for the words "Part II of the Social Security and Housing Benefits Act 1982" there shall be substituted the words "Part II of the Social Security Act 1986".

Magistrates' Courts Act 1980 (c. 43)

54. The following paragraph shall be added after subsection 1(*l*) of section 65 of the Magistrates' Courts Act 1980 (domestic proceedings)—

"(*m*) section 24 or 25 of the Social Security Act 1986; ".

Civil Jurisdiction and Judgments Act 1982 (c. 27)

55. In paragraph 5 of Schedule 5 to the Civil Jurisdiction and Judgments Act 1982 (proceedings excluded from Schedule 4)—

(*a*) in sub-paragraph (*c*), after "1976," there shall be inserted the words "section 24 of the Social Security Act 1986, or any enactment applying in Northern Ireland and corresponding to it," ; and

(*b*) in sub-paragraph (*d*), after "1976," there shall be inserted the words "section 25 of the Social Security Act 1986 or any enactment applying in Northern Ireland and corresponding to it,".

Legal Aid Act 1982 (c. 44)

56. In section 7(8) of the Legal Aid Act 1982 (legal aid contribution orders) for the words from " supplementary benefit " to the end there shall be substituted the words " income support or family credit under the Social Security Act 1986.".

Transport Act 1982 (c. 49)

57. In section 70(2)(*b*) of the Transport Act 1982 (payments in respect of applicants for exemption from wearing seat belts) for the words from " of " to " and " there shall be substituted the words " of income support or family credit and ".

Housing Act 1985 (c.68)

58. In subsection (2)(*b*) of section 425 of the Housing Act 1985 (the local contribution differential) for the words " section 32 of the Social Security and Housing Benefits Act 1982 " there shall be substituted the words " section 30 of the Social Security Act 1986 ".

59. In Item 4 in Part I of Schedule 14 to that Act (items to be credited to the Housing Revenue Account) for the words " Social Security and Housing Benefits Act 1982 " there shall be substituted the words " Social Security Act 1986 ".

60. In paragraph 3 of Part IV of that Schedule (rate fund contributions to the Housing Revenue Account) for the words " section 34(1) of the Social Security and Housing Benefits Act 1982 " there shall be substituted the words " section 30(6) of the Social Security Act 1986 ".

Legal Aid (Scotland) Act 1986 (c.47)

61. In section 8(*b*) (availability of legal advice and assistance) and section 11(2) (clients' contributions) of the Legal Aid (Scotland) Act 1986, for the words from " supplementary " to " 1970 " there shall be substituted the words " income suport or family credit ".

PART III

BENEFITS UNDER SOCIAL SECURITY ACT 1975

Social Security Act 1975 (c. 14)

62. The Social Security Act 1975 shall have effect subject to the amendments specified in paragraphs 63 to 66 below.

63. In section 12(1) (descriptions of contributory benefits) the following sub-paragraph shall be substituted for sub-paragraph (i) of paragraph (*e*)—

" (i) widow's payment,".

64. In section 13 (contribution conditions) in subsection (1), in the Table headed " Other benefits " the following entry shall be inserted before the entry relating to widowed mother's allowance—

" Widow's payment   ...".

65. The following entry shall be inserted in section 167(1)(*a*) of that Act (regulations subject to affirmative Parliamentary procedure) immediately after the entry relating to section 20(3)—

" section 61(3) (constant attendance allowance) ; "

66. In Schedule 3 (contribution conditions)—

(*a*) in paragraph 4(1) for the words preceding paragraph (*a*) there shall be substituted the words—

" Widow's payment

4.—(1) The contribution condition for a widow's payment is that—"

(*b*) " payment " shall be substituted for " allowance "—

(i) in sub-paragraph (2)(*b*) of paragraph 8 ; and

(ii) in the second place where it occurs in sub-paragraph (3) of that paragraph ; and

(*c*) the following paragraph shall be substituted for paragraph 13—

" 13. Where a woman claims a widow's payment, the contributor concerned for the purposes of the claim shall be deemed to satisfy the contribution condition for the payment if on a claim made in the past for any short-term benefit he has satisfied the first contribution condition for the benefit, by virtue of paragraph 8 above, with contributions of a class relevant to widow's payment.".

Industrial Injuries and Diseases (Old Cases) Act 1975 (c. 16)

67. The words following " pension rate " shall be omitted from sections 2(6)(*b*) and 7(2)(*c*) (weekly rates of benefit) of the Industrial Injuries and Diseases (Old Cases) Act 1975.

68.—(1) In section 4(8)(*a*) of that Act (parliamentary procedure for making of schemes) for the words " an up-rating order under the Social Security Act " there shall be substituted the words " any order or regulations under the Social Security Acts 1975 to 1986 ".

(2) In section 7 of that Act (amount of benefit)—

(*a*) in subsection (3), the following paragraph shall be substituted for paragraph (*d*)—

" (*d*) where the person is treated under the provisions of the scheme as residing with his or her spouse or contributing at a weekly rate of not less than the relevant amount towards the maintenance of his or her spouse, by the relevant amount (that is to say, an amount equal to any increase which would be payable under section 44

of that Act in respect of the spouse if the person were
entitled to sickness benefit)." ; and

(*b*) in subsection (4), the following paragraph shall be substituted for the paragraph set out in that subsection—

" (*d*) where the person is treated under the provisions of
the scheme as residing with his or her spouse or contributing at a weekly rate of not less than the relevant amount
towards the maintenance of his or her spouse, by the
relevant amount (that is to say, an amount equal to any
increase which would be payable under section 66 of that
Act in respect of the spouse if the person were entitled
to disablement pension plus unemployability supplement).".

Social Security Pensions Act 1975 (c. 60)

69. In section 13(3) of the Social Security Pensions Act 1975 (rate
of widowed mother's allowance and widow's pension) for " 50 "
there shall be substituted " 55 ".

70. In section 15 of that Act (invalidity pension for widows)—

(*a*) in subsection (1)—

(i) the following paragraphs shall be substituted for
paragraphs (*a*) and (*b*)—

" (*a*) is not entitled to a widowed mother's allowance
on her late husband's death or subsequently
ceases to be entitled to such an allowance ; and

(*b*) is incapable of work at the time when he died or
when she subsequently ceases to be so entitled ;" ;

(ii) in paragraph (*c*), for " 40 " there shall be substituted " 45 " ;

(*b*) in subsection (2)(*a*), for the words from " she " to the end
there shall be substituted the words " her late husband died
or she subsequently ceased to be entitled to a widowed
mother's allowance ; " ; and

(*c*) in subsection (4)(*a*), for " 50 " there shall be substituted " 55 ".

Part IV

Statutory Maternity Pay, Statutory Sick Pay Etc.

Income and Corporation Taxes Act 1970 (c. 10)

71. At the end of section 219A of the Income and Corporation
Taxes Act 1970 (which charges certain payments to income tax under
Schedule E) there shall be added " and

(*d*) payments of statutory maternity pay under Part V of the
Social Security Act 1986 or, in Northern Ireland, any corresponding provision contained in an Order in Council under
the Northern Ireland Act 1974.".

Social Security Act 1975 (c. 14)

72. The words " (other than maternity allowance) " shall be inserted—

(*a*) after the words " that subsection ", in subsection (2) of section 13 of the Social Security Act 1975 ; and

(*b*) after the words " for benefit ", in subsection (8) of that section.

73. In section 122(4) of that Act for the words " either or both those Funds " there shall be substituted the words " that Fund ".

Social Security (Miscellaneous Provisions) Act 1977 (c. 5)

74. In section 18(2)(*c*) of the Social Security (Miscellaneous Provisions) Act 1977 (certain sums to be earnings for social security purposes) for the words " that Act " there shall be substituted the
words " the Employment Protection (Consolidation) Act 1978 ".

Employment Protection (Consolidation) Act 1978 (c. 44)

75. In section 33 of the Employment Protection (Consolidation) Act 1978 (right to return to work) in subsections (3) and (4) for the word " rights " there shall be substituted the word " right " and in subsection (5) for the words " either of the rights " there shall be substituted the words " the right ".

76. In subsection (4) of section 123 of that Act (payment of unpaid contributions to pension schemes) for the words " maternity pay " there shall be substituted the words " statutory sick pay, statutory maternity pay under Part V of the Social Security Act 1986, maternity pay under Part III of this Act ".

Social Security and Housing Benefits Act 1982 (c. 24)

77. The following subsection shall be substituted for section 3(9) of the Social Security and Housing Benefits Act 1982 (definitions relating to period of entitlement to statutory sick pay)—

" (9) In this section—

" confinement " is to be construed in accordance with section 50 of the Social Security Act 1986 ; and

" disqualifying period " means—

(*a*) in relation to a woman entitled to statutory maternity pay, the maternity pay period ; and

(*b*) in relation to a woman entitled to maternity allowance, the maternity allowance period ;

" maternity allowance period " has the meaning assigned to it by section 22(2) of the principal Act ; and

" maternity pay period " has the meaning assigned to it by section 47(1) of the Social Security Act 1986.".

78. The following paragraph shall be inserted before paragraph (*a*) of section 45(2) of that Act (Parliamentary control of subordinate legislation)—

" (*za*) regulations under section 7 of this Act ; ".

Insolvency Act 1985 (c. 65)

79. In paragraph 3(2)(*d*) of Part II of Schedule 4 to the Insolvency Act 1985 (preferential debts) the words from the beginning to " 1982 " shall cease to have effect.

Bankruptcy (Scotland) Act 1985 (c. 66)

80. Paragraph 9(2)(*d*) of Schedule 3 to the Bankruptcy (Scotland) Act 1985 (preferential debts) shall cease to have effect.

Wages Act 1986 (c.48)

81. In subsection (1)(*f*) of section 7 of the Wages Act 1986 (meaning of " wages ") for the words " maternity pay under Part III of the 1978 Act " there shall be substituted the words " statutory maternity pay under the Social Security Act 1986 ".

PART V

COMMON PROVISIONS

Social Security Act 1973 (c. 38)

82. In section 68(1) of the Social Security Act 1973 (submission to Occupational Pensions Board of proposals to make regulations) for the word " Where " there shall be substituted the words " Subject to section 61 of the Social Security Act 1986, where ".

Social Security Act 1975 (c. 14)

83. In subsection (6)(*aa*) of section 14 of the Social Security Act 1975 (unemployment benefit and sickness benefit) and in subsection (4)(*aa*) of section 15 of that Act (invalidity pension) for the words " 126A of this Act " there shall be substituted the words " 63 (1)(*d*) of the Social Security Act 1986 ".

84. In subsection (1) of section 28 of that Act (Category A retirement pension) the words from " (subject " to " rule)) " shall be omitted.

85. The following subsection shall be substituted for subsection (3) of section 90 of that Act (obligations of claimant)—

" (3) The regulations relevant under subsection (2) above are—

(*a*) those made by virtue of the following provisions of this Chapter, namely—

(i) section 88(*a*), and

(ii) section 89(1) and (2) ; and

(*b*) those made by virtue of section 51(1)(*h*), (*k*) and (*l*) of the Social Security Act 1986.".

86. In section 141(2) (reference of proposals to make regulations to Industrial Injuries Advisory Council) for the word " Where " there shall be substituted the words " Subject to section 61 of the Social Security Act 1986, where ".

87. The following section shall be substituted for section 165A of that Act—

" General provision as to necessity of claim for entitlement to benefit.

165A.—(1) Except in such cases as may be prescribed, no person shall be entitled to any benefit unless, in addition to any other conditions relating to that benefit being satisfied—

(*a*) he makes a claim for it in the prescribed manner and within the prescribed time ; or

(*b*) by virtue of regulations made under section 51

of the Social Security Act 1986 he is treated as making a claim for it.

(2) Where under subsection (1) above a person is required to make a claim or to be treated as making a claim for a benefit in order to be entitled to it—

(a) if the benefit is a widow's payment, she shall not be entitled to it in respect of a death occurring more than twelve months before the date on which the claim is made or treated as made; and

(b) if the benefit is any other benefit, except disablement benefit or reduced earnings allowance, the person shall not be entitled to it in respect of any period more than twelve months before that date.".

88. The words ", reduced earnings allowance" shall be inserted in section 165A(3)(c), as originally enacted, after the words " disablement benefit ".

89. In section 167(3) of that Act (parliamentary procedure) for the words ", 123A or 126A or an up-rating order " there shall be substituted the words " or 123A ".

90. In paragraph 8 of Schedule 16 (exemption in respect of up-rating regulations from requirements to consult Industrial Injuries Advisory Council) for the words from " one or more " to the end there shall be substituted the words " one or more of the following provisions—

(a) section 120 and 122 of this Act; and

(b) section 63 of the Social Security Act 1986.".

Social Security Pensions Act 1975 (c. 60)

91. In section 23 of the Social Security Pensions Act 1975 (increase of long-term benefits)—

(a) in subsections (2) and (3), for the words " the said section 124 " there shall be substituted the words " section 63 of the Social Security Act 1986 ";

(b) in subsection (2), for the words " subsection (1)(b) above " there shall be substituted the words " section 63(1)(b) of that Act "; and

(c) in subsection (3), for the words " subsection (1)(c) or (d) above " there shall be substituted the words " section 63(1)(c) or (d) of that Act ".

92. In section 24(1)(a) of that Act (graduated retirement benefit) for the words " 124 to 126 of the principal Act " there shall be substituted the words " sections 63 and 64 of the Social Security Act 1986 ".

93. In subsection (1) of section 59 of that Act (official pension) for the words " that section " there shall be substituted the words " section 63 of the Social Security Act 1986 ".

94. In section 61(2) of that Act (consultation about regulations)—

   (a) for the word " Where " there shall be substituted the words " Subject to section 61 of the Social Security Act 1986, where " ; and

   (b) after the words " of this Act " there shall be inserted the words " or of Part I of the Social Security Act 1986 ".

95. In Schedule 1 to that Act (deferred retirement)—

   (a) in paragraphs 2(5) and 4(3)(b), for the words " 124 of the principal Act " there shall be substituted the words " 63 of the Social Security Act 1986 " ; and

   (b) in paragraph 4A(3)(a), for the words " 126A of the principal Act " there shall be substituted the words " 63(1)(d) of the Social Security Act 1986 ".

Child Benefit Act 1975 (c. 61)

96. At the end of subsection (1) of section 6 of the Child Benefit Act 1975 (child benefit claims and payments) there shall be added the words " and within the prescribed time".

97. In paragraph 1 of Schedule 3 to that Act (increases in rate of benefit), after the word " Act " there shall be inserted the words " or section 63 of the Social Security Act 1986 ".

Social Security Act 1980 (c. 30)

98. In section 10 of the Social Security Act 1980 (consultation with Social Security Advisory Committee on proposals for regulations)—

   (a) in subsection (1), after the word " subsection " there shall be inserted the words " and to section 61 of the Social Security Act 1986 " ; and

   (b) in subsection (9), after the word " section " there shall be inserted the words " or section 61 of the Social Security Act 1986 ".

99. In paragraph 12(2) of Schedule 3 to that Act (regulations not requiring submission to Social Security Advisory Committee) for the words from " sections of " to the end there shall be substituted the words " provisions—

   (a) section 120, 122 or 123A of the principal Act ;

   (b) section 63 of the Social Security Act 1986,

or contained in a statutory rule which states that it contains only provisions in consequence of an order under section 120 of the Social Security (Northern Ireland) Act 1975 or any enactment apply- 1975 c. 15. ing in Northern Ireland and corresponding to section 63 of the Social Security Act 1986.".

Social Security Act 1985 (c. 53)

100. In section 9(9) of the Social Security Act 1985 (abatement of invalidity allowance) for the words " sections 124 and 126A of the Social Security Act 1975 " there shall be substituted the words 1975 c. 14. " section 63 of the Social Security Act 1986 ".

Part VI

Miscellaneous

Income and Corporation Taxes Act 1970 (c. 10)

101. In section 219 of the Income and Corporation Taxes Act 1970 (taxation of benefits)—

> (*a*) in subsection (1), for the words, " maternity benefit " there shall be substituted the words " maternity allowance, widow's payments " ; and

> (*b*) in subsection (2), for the words " in respect of a family income supplement under the Family Income Supplements Act 1970 or the Family Income Supplements Act (Northern Ireland) 1971 " there shall be substituted the words " of family credit under the Social Security Act 1986 or any corresponding enactment applying to Northern Ireland,".

1970 c. 55.
1971 c. 8.
(N.I.).

Attachment of Earnings Act 1971 (c. 32)

102. In section 24(2)(*c*) of the Aattachment of Earnings Act 1971 (social security benefits etc. not earnings for purposes of Act) for the words from " of " to the end there shall be substituted " enactment relating to social security ; ".

National Insurance Act 1974 (c. 14)

Social Security Act 1980 (c. 30)

Social Security Act 1985 (c. 53)

103. The words " the Social Security Acts 1975 to 1986 " shall be substituted—

> (*a*) for the words " the Social Security Act 1975 " in section 6(1) of the National Insurance Act 1974 ;

> (*b*) in the Social Security Act 1980—

>> (i) in section 9(7), for the words " the Social Security Acts 1975 to 1985 " in both places where they occur ; and

>> (ii) in section 18(1), for the words " the Social Security Acts 1975 to 1982 " ; and

> (*c*) for the words " the Social Security Acts 1975 to 1985 " in section 5 of the Social Security Act 1985.

Social Security Act 1975 (c. 14)

104. In section 4(6) of the Social Security Act 1975 (incidence of Class 1 contributions) after the word " under " there shall be inserted the words " subsection (7) below or under ".

Supplementary Benefits Act 1976 (c. 71)

105. In section 8 of the Supplementary Benefits Act 1976 (persons affected by trade disputes)—

> (*a*) in subsection (1), the following words shall be substituted for the words from the beginning to " period ", in the second place where it occurs—

> " So long as this section applies to a person, his requirements " ; and

(*b*) the following subsections shall be substituted for subsection   Sᴄʜ. 10
(2)—

     " (2) This section applies to a person—

         (*a*) who is disqualified under section 19 of the Social 1975 c. 14.
            Security Act 1975 for receiving unemployment
            benefit ; or

         (*b*) who would be so disqualified if otherwise en-
            titled to that benefit,

except during any period shown by the person to be a
period of incapacity for work by reason of disease or
bodily or mental disablement or to be within the maternity period.

     (2A) In subsection (2) above " the maternity period "
means the period commencing at the beginning of the
sixth week before the expected week of confinement and
ending at the end of the seventh week after the week in
which confinement takes place.".

Social Security Act 1980 (c. 30)

106. The following sub-paragraph shall be inserted after paragraph
13(1) of Schedule 3 to the Social Security Act 1980 (regulations not
requiring prior submission to Social Security Advisory Committee)—

     " (1A) Regulations under section 3(2)(*a*) of the Pensions Act
(which provides for enabling women to continue to make contributions at reduced rate).".

107. The reference to section 9 of the Social Security and Housing 1982 c. 24.
Benefits Act 1982 in paragraph 15A of that Schedule shall include
a reference to subsection (1A) of that section.

Forfeiture Act 1982 (c. 34)

108. In section 4 of the Forfeiture Act 1982—

     (*a*) in subsection (4), for " and (3) " there shall be substituted
        " to (3A) " ; and

     (*b*) in subsection (5), for the words from " the Family Income 1970 c. 55.
        Supplements Act 1970 " to " the Social Security Act 1980 " 1980 c. 30.
        there shall be substituted the words—

           " the Child Benefit Act 1975,   1975 c. 61.

        the Social Security Acts 1975 to 1986.".

SCHEDULE 11

REPEALS

Chapter	Short title	Extent of repeal
11 & 12 Geo. 6. c. 29.	National Assistance Act 1948.	In section 43(6), the words ", whether before or after the commencement of the Supplementary Benefits Act 1976,". In section 50(4), the words " or subsection (3) " and the words from " less " to the end. Section 53.
1965 c. 55.	Statute Law Revision (Consequential Repeals) Act 1965.	The whole Act.
1966 c. 20.	Supplementary Benefit Act 1966.	Section 26.
1968 c. 49.	Social Work (Scotland) Act 1968.	In section 28(2), the words " and not reimbursed under section 32 of the Social Security Act 1975 ".
1970 c. 10.	Income and Corporation Taxes Act 1970.	In section 219(1), the words " death grant ". In section 219A(1)(b), the word " and ".
1970 c. 55.	Family Income Supplements Act 1970.	The whole Act.
1971 c. 32.	Attachment of Earnings Act 1971.	Schedule 4.
1972 c. 70.	Local Government Act 1972.	In section 119(2), the words from " having " to the end.
1972 c. 75.	Pensioners and Family Income Supplement Payments Act 1972.	The whole Act.
1972 c. 80.	Pensioners' Payments and National Insurance Contributions Act 1972.	The whole Act.
1973 c. 38.	Social Security Act 1973.	Section 92(3) and (4). In section 99(1), the definition of requisite benefits. Schedule 23.
1973 c. 61.	Pensioners' Payments and National Insurance Act 1973.	The whole Act.
1974 c. 14.	National Insurance Act 1974.	In section 6(1), the words " the Supplementary Benefits Act 1976, the Family Income Supplements Act 1970," and the words " or the Social Security and Housing Benefits Act 1982 ".
1974 c. 54.	Pensioners' Payments Act 1974.	The whole Act.
1975 c. 14.	Social Security Act 1975.	In section 1(1)(b), the words " and the Maternity Pay Fund ".

Chapter	Short title	Extent of repeal
		In section 12, in subsection (1), paragraph (*h*), in subsection (2), the words " and widow's allowance " and subsection (3).
		In section 13, in subsection (1), the entries relating to widow's allowance and death grant, subsection (5)(*a*) and subsection (5A).
		Section 21.
		In section 25(3), the words " and for which she is not entitled to a widow's allowance ".
		In section 26(3), the words " a widow's allowance or ".
		In section 28(1), the words from " (subject " to " rule)) ".
		Section 32.
		Section 33(1)(*a*) to (*c*).
		Section 34(2).
		In section 37(3), the words from "and a woman" to the end.
		Section 37A(4) and (7).
		Section 41(2)(*e*) and (2C).
		Section 50(2) and (5).
		Section 57(5).
		Sections 58 and 59.
		Section 60.
		Section 62.
		Sections 64 to 75.
		Sections 79 to 81.
		In section 82, subsections (3) and (4) and subsection (6)(*a*).
		In section 84, subsection (3) and in subsection (5), the references to sections 65 and 66.
		Section 86.
		In section 88(*a*), the words from " or ", in the first place where it occurs, to " prescribed ", in the third place where it occurs.
		In section 90, in subsection (2)(*a*), the words from " (including " to the end and in subsection (3), the references to sections 79 and 81.
		In section 91, subsection (1)(*b*)(i) and in subsection (2), the words " section 58 (unemployability supplement)," and the words from " section 64 " to the end.

Chapter	Short title	Extent of repeal
		Section 92.
		Section 95.
		In section 100, in subsection (1), the words " adversely to the claimant " and subsections (5) and (6).
		In section 101(3)(c), the words " or, in relation to industrial death benefit, the deceased ".
		In section 104(1A), the words "in prescribed circumstances".
		Section 106(3).
		In section 107, in subsection (4), the words ", whether or not the claimant is the person at whose instance the declaration was made " and in subsection (6), the words " by fresh evidence " and paragraph (b).
		In section 110(1), the words " by fresh evidence ".
		Section 114(3) and (4).
		In section 117, subsection (4) and in subsection (5), paragraph (a) and the word " and " immediately following it.
		In section 119, subsections (1) to (2A), in subsection (3)(b), the words " or out of a requirement to repay any amount by virtue of subsection (2A) above ", subsection (4)(b) to (d) and subsections (5) and (6).
		In section 122(4), the words " or the Maternity Pay Fund ".
		Sections 124 to 126A.
		In section 134(5)(b), the words from " and the Maternity Pay Fund " to " determine ".
		In section 135, subsections (2)(g) and (6).
		Section 136.
		In section 141(2), the words from " unless " to the end.
		In section 143(1), the words " relating to social security ".
		Sections 144 and 145.
		In section 146, in subsection (1), the words " under Part III of the Pensions Act " and subsections (3)(c) and (5).
		Section 147.

Chapter	Short title	Extent of repeal
		In section 151(1), the words " under Part III of the Pensions Act ".
		In section 152(8), the words " of the Pensions Act (including in particular sections 47 and 64(3)) " and the words " under that Act ".
		Section 164.
		In Schedule 3, in Part I, paragraph 7 and, in Part II, in paragraph 8(2), in paragraph (*a*), the words " other than a widow's allowance ", in paragraph 8(3), the words " or a maternity allowance," in paragraphs 9 and 10, the words " (other than a widow's allowance) " and paragraph 12.
		In Schedule 4, in Part I, paragraph 5, Part II, in Part IV, paragraph 4 and in Part V, paragraphs 2, 4 to 6 and 10 to 15.
		Schedule 5.
		In Schedule 8, paragraph (*b*) of the proviso to paragraph 5 and the word " and " immediately preceding it.
		Schedule 9.
		Schedule 14.
		In Schedule 16, paragraphs 3 and 4.
		In Schedule 20, the definitions of " The deceased " and " Industrial death benefit ", in the definition of " Relative ", the reference to sections 66(8) and 72(6), in the definition of " Short-term benefit " the words " and widow's allowance ", the definitions of " Unemployability supplement " and " Up-rating order", and in the definition of " Week ", the reference to section 64.
1975 c. 16.	Industrial Injuries and Diseases (Old Cases) Act 1975.	In section 4(4), paragraph (*c*)(ii) and the word " or " immediately preceding it.
		Section 9(3).
		Section 10.
1975 c. 18.	Social Security (Consequential Provisions) Act 1975.	In Schedule 2, paragraphs 5, 35, 41 and 44.
		In Schedule 3, paragraph 18.

Chapter	Short title	Extent of repeal
1975 c. 60.	Social Security Pensions Act 1975.	In section 6, in subsection (2), the words from " or " to the end, in subsection (5), the words " Subject to subsection (5A) below," and subsection (5A). In section 19(2), the words " and (3)(*b*)." Section 22(3) and (5). Section 23(1) and (5). Section 30(2). In section 32(4), the words " relating to the scheme or its management ". Section 33(1)(*a*) and (4). Section 34. In section 36, subsections (2), (4) and (5), in subsection (6), the words " Subject to the following provisions of this section ", subsection (7), in subsection (8), the words from " but the scheme " to the end and subsection (9). Section 37. In section 39, subsections (2), (3) and (4)(*a*). Section 41(4). In section 44A(1)(*b*) and (4), the words " to requisite benefits ". Section 46. Section 49(3) and (7). Section 52D(2) and (3). Section 56K(4). In section 66(1), the definition of " requisite benefits " and, in the definition of " resources ", the words " (whether requisite benefits or other benefits) ". In Schedule 1A, in paragraph 12, in sub-paragraph (3), the words " Subject to sub-paragraph (4) below," and sub-paragraph (4). In Schedule 2, paragraph 4. In Schedule 4, paragraphs 14 and 17, in paragraph 31 the definition of " requisite benefits " and paragraphs 32(*a*), 41, 42 and 51.
1975 c. 61.	Child Benefit Act 1975.	Section 5(5). Section 6(2), (4) and (5). Sections 7 and 8. Section 9(1). Sections 10 and 11. In section 15(1), the words " relating to child benefit ".

Chapter	Short title	Extent of repeal
		Section 17(3) to (6).
		In section 24(1), in the definition of " recognised educational establishment ", the words from " and " to the end.
		In Schedule 4, paragraphs 3 to 6, 11, 27, 29, 31 and 33.
1975 c. 71.	Employment Protection Act 1975.	In section 40, subsections (2) and (4).
1976 c. 36.	Adoption Act 1976.	Section 47(3).
1976 c. 71.	Supplementary Benefits Act 1976.	Sections 1 to 21.
		Sections 24 to 27.
		Sections 31 to 34.
		Schedule 1.
		In Schedule 5, in paragraph 1(2), the words from the beginning to " and " in the first place where it occurs.
		In Schedule 7, paragraphs 1(b) and (d), 3(a), 5, 19,21,23, 24, 31, 33 and 37.
1977 c. 5.	Social Security (Miscellaneous Provisions) Act 1977.	Section 9.
		Section 17(2).
		In section 18, in subsection (1), in paragraph (a) the words " and the Supplementary Benefits Act 1976 " and paragraphs (c) and in subsection (2) paragraphs (a) and (b).
		Section 19.
		In section 22, in subsection (2), the references to sections 24(2) and 37(3)(b) of the Social Security Act 1975, and subsection (16).
1977 c. 51.	Pensioners' Payments Act 1977.	The whole Act.
1978 c. 44.	Employment Protection (Consolidation) Act 1978	In section 33, subsection (1)(a) and the word " and " immediately following it, in subsection (3), paragraph (c) and in paragraph (d) the words "in the case of the right to return" and in subsection (4), the words " to return ".
		Sections 34 to 44.
		Section 122(4)(e).
		In section 123(5), the words " occupational pension ".
		In section 127(3), the word " such " in the second place where it occurs.
		In section 132, in subsection (1)(b) ",III " and in subsection (6), the definition of " supplementary benefit ".
		In section 133(1)(a), ",33 ".

Chapter	Short title	Extent of repeal
		In section 138, in subsection (1) the words " (except section 44) ", and in subsection (5) the words " (except section 44(3) and (4)) ". In section 139(1), the words " (except section 44) ". In section 153(1) the definitions of " maternity pay ", " Maternity Pay Fund " and " maternity pay rebate ". In section 155(1), the words " 44 to ". Section 156(1). Section 157(2)(*a*) and the word " and " immediately following it. In Schedule 14, paragraph 7(1) (*d*). In Schedule 15, paragraph 7 and the heading immediately preceding it.
1978 c. 58.	Pensioners' Payments Act 1978.	The whole Act.
1979 c. 18.	Social Security Act 1979.	Section 3(2). Sections 6 to 8. Sections 12 and 13. In Schedule 3, paragraphs 1, 2, 9, 16 and 24 to 27.
1979 c. 41.	Pneumoconiosis etc. (Workers' Compensation) Act 1979.	In section 2(3), the words " industrial death benefit under section 76 of the Social Security Act 1975, or ".
1979 c. 48.	Pensioners' Payments and Social Security Act 1979.	The whole Act.
1980 c. 5.	Child Care Act 1980.	In section 25(2), the words from " less " to the end.
1980 c. 30.	Social Security Act 1980.	Section 1. Section 4(4). In section 5, in subsection (1) the words from " and in subsection (2) ", in paragraph (i), to the end of the subsection and subsections (2) to (4). Section 7. In section 8, in subsection (1), the words " or 7 ". In section 9(7), the words " the Family Income Supplements Act 1970 " and the words " and the Supplementary Benefits Act 1976 ".

Chapter	Short title	Extent of repeal
		In section 10, in subsection (2) and in subsection (7), in the first place where they occur, the words " the Secretary of State or, as the case may be," and in subsection (7), the words " to the Secretary of State, or as the case may be," and paragraph (*a*).
		In section 14, subsection (6).
		Section 15.
		In section 17(2), the words from " a tribunal " to the end.
		In section 18, in subsection (1), the words " the Family Income Supplements Act 1970;", the words " the Supplementary Benefits Act 1976" and the word " and " immediately preceding them.
		Section 20(3).
		In Schedule 1, in paragraph 9, the words " or section 95(1)(*b*) or (*c*) " and paragraphs 10 and 12.
		In Schedule 2, paragraphs 1 to 20, and 22 to 30.
		In Schedule 3, in Part II, paragraphs 11, 15, 15B and 16 to 18.
1980 c. 39.	Social Security (No. 2) Act 1980.	Sections 1 and 2.
		In section 4(2), the words " and no earnings-related addition to a widow's allowance ".
		Section 6.
1981 c. 33.	Social Security Act 1981.	Section 1.
		Section 4.
		In Schedule 1, paragraphs 1, 2, 3(*b*), 4, 5, 8 and 9.
1982 c. 24.	Social Security and Housing Benefits Act 1982.	Section 7(3) to (10).
		Section 8.
		Section 9(8) to (10).
		Sections 11 to 16.
		Sections 19 to 21.
		Section 25.
		Part II.
		Section 38.
		Section 41.
		Section 42(1) and (2).
		Section 44(1)(*a*) and (*f*).
		In section 45, in subsection (1), the words from " and any power " to the end, in subsection (2), in paragraph (*a*), the words " 7 or " and paragraphs (*b*) and (*c*) and subsection (3).

Chapter	Short title	Extent of repeal
		In section 47 in the definition of " benefit ", the words " Part II and ". In Schedule 2, paragraph 6. Schedule 3. In Schedule 4, paragraphs 2, 4, 5, 14, 19, 22 to 28, 35(1) and (2) and 38.
1983 c. 36.	Social Security and Housing Benefits Act 1983.	The whole Act.
1983 c. 41.	Health and Social Services and Social Security Adjudications Act 1983.	Section 19(2). In Schedule 8, Parts III and IV and paragraphs 18 and 31(3). In Schedule 9, paragraph 20.
1984 c. 22.	Public Health (Control of Disease) Act 1984.	In section 46(5), the words from " less " to the end.
1984 c. 48.	Health and Social Security Act 1984.	Section 22. In section 27(2), the words " 22 and ". In Schedule 4, in paragraph 3 the entry relating to section 79 and paragraphs 12 and 14. In Schedule 5, paragraphs 4 to 6.
1985 c. 53.	Social Security Act 1985.	Sections 15 to 17. Section 22. Section 27(8)(*e*). In section 32(2), the words " section 15 " and the words " section 22(1)(*b*) and (*c*) and (2) ". In Schedule 4, paragraph 2. In Schedule 5, paragraphs 6, 7, 10, 16, 19, 28, 37 and 38.
1985 c. 65.	Insolvency Act 1985.	In Part II of Schedule 4, the words in paragraph 3(2)(*d*) from the beginning to " 1982 ".
1985 c. 66.	Bankruptcy (Scotland) Act 1985.	In Schedule 3, paragraph 9(2) (*d*).
1986 c. 9.	Law Reform (Parent and Child) (Scotland) Act 1986.	In Schedule 1, paragraph 16. In Schedule 2, the entry relating to the Supplementary Benefits Act 1976.

PRODUCED IN THE UK FOR W.J. SHARP, CB
Controller and Chief Executive of Her Majesty's Stationery Office
and Queen's Printer of Acts of Parliament
LONDON: PUBLISHED BY HER MAJESTY'S STATIONERY OFFICE

PS 6352721 Dd.905450 C40 12/86 CCP